Palmistry or Chiromancy Explained

The Ultimate Palmistry Guide for Beginners

Chiromancy Overview, Basics of Palmistry, Palm Lines, Mounts, Indications, History, Do's and Don'ts, and More!

By Riley Star

Foreword

Palmistry is indeed a very interesting and intriguing yet compelling subject that enables a person to understand the nature of another person and even foretell or perhaps take a peek at one's future just by simply looking at the palm of their hands. It is in fact a fascinating study, but it is not as simple as you think.

One cannot master the art of palm reading easily or be proficient in a quick period of time just by studying the basics of palmistry or reading a book about it. Like any other things, time, practice, willingness and experience will make you better and more proficient. Nevertheless, a book like this is a start, because it could provide you with the basic knowledge, instructions and work structure that you will need to help you become an 'expert' palm reader.

Fortunately, thanks to the advent of the internet, you can now study palmistry without going to 'weird' fortune tellers or paying for their service to learn the tricks of the trade. If you or any of your friends and family is interested about this subject, this book will provide you with a wealth of information about Palmistry or otherwise known as Chiromancy; its basics, its significance, its rich history, the different interpretations, the different meanings, its logical structure and so much more. Get ready to understand your life at present and be able to 'predict' your future just like many ancient palm readers that came before you!

Table of Contents

Introduction

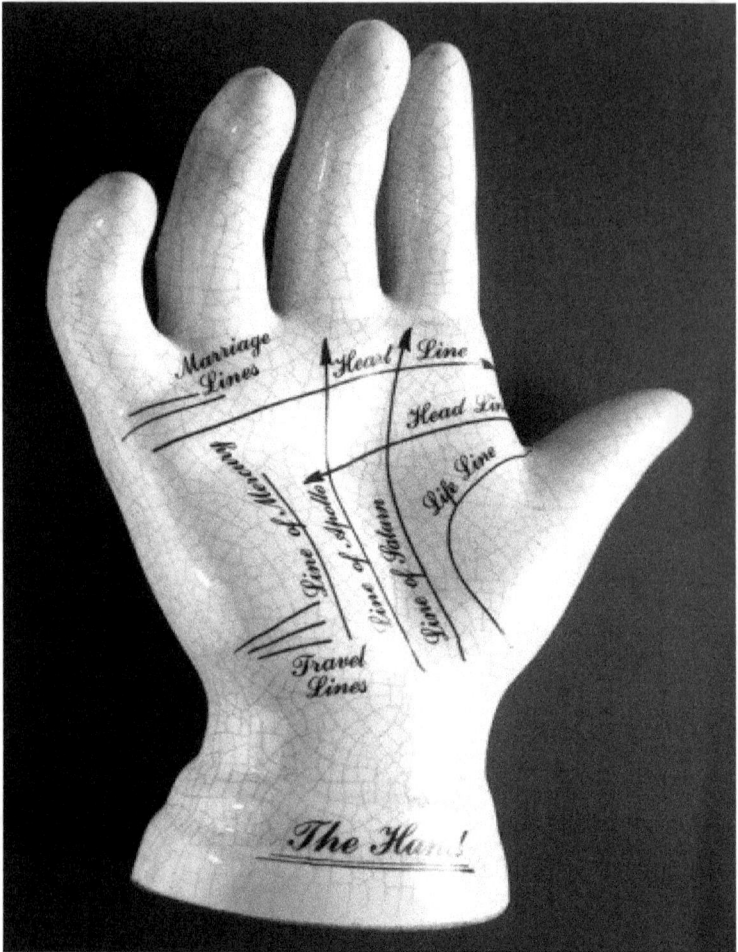

In United States, many people are interested in studying palmistry or chiromancy. The group of people who tries to understand how palmistry works usually comes from the business field, which includes organization leaders and entrepreneurs. According to many palmistry experts, these group of people wanted to study and grasp the basics of palm reading because it could help them in their business careers, how they deal with people especially during negotiations, how they hire employees, and basically how to assess any person that comes in contact with them in order to reveal a person's true nature or character that is beyond their own judgment.

However, for a student to avoid being confused with the complexities and rules of how palmistry works, you need to make sure that you study it in a logical manner so that you could build your structure or process from there.

If you want to become a master in this field of study you need to follow a certain framework which could guide you in palm reading. All palm experts have a structure way of working; they don't just look at a hand and read whatever attracts their attention. Usually palm reading experts examine all aspects of the hand first such as the fingers, the shapes, the lines, the texture, the firmness or softness, the color, and basically the overall palm so that they can have an overview of the "bigger picture," before getting into details and "connecting the dots" for the purpose of interpretation.

Before reading and learning the basics of palmistry or how it works, it's imperative that any student first have an open mindset or a kind of thinking that accepts possibilities. If you think you are the kind of person that can't accept things without proof or you always doubt on how things work, then I suggest that you better stop reading this now and just pick up another book, perhaps one that has a scientific theme.

This is because palm reading, in spite of its long history, is not and will never be a fact or an exact science. There is no proof that it works (or not), and it is definitely not backed by scientific tests which is why the subject can only be considered as hypothetical, but that doesn't mean that palmistry is not entirely true or false for that matter. Perhaps it could be something that our ancestors developed many centuries ago to explain strange phenomena or simply developed out of boredom, no one knows for sure.

It is an art that withstood the test of time, a practice that has been passed on for many generations and in one way or another affected how people live their lives. There could be instances where one can relate a personal situation to that of the prediction done through palm reading but it could be purely coincidental or it could be real, who knows? Keeping an open mind while studying this art is essential for you to truly understand how the system works. Nevertheless, whether people or experts consider chiromancy as something real or just a product of pure imagination, the present or the future as well as the nature of one's character is all in the mind. Always remember that your fate lies not on what is 'written' in the palm of your hands, it lies upon you. As what W.E. Henley famously said, "I'm the master of my fate; I'm the captain of my soul."

Chapter One: Understanding Palmistry

The first chapter is dedicated to some general knowledge of how palmistry came about. Before we deal with its system or process, it's important to know the scope of the topic first. Some people becomes very confused about what a palmist can and cannot do, or how palmistry works in general, because of what they read off of magazines, press, social media or internet blogs, or what they've heard from various stories passed on from one family to another about predictions of ones future and the nature of palm reading. These are main causes of confusion because our mind tends to formulate opinions or perceptions based on what we see or hear. Unfortunately, for a lot of people palmistry is something that is unrealistic.

Again, we cannot tell for sure if it actually works or not because there are also instances or situations where we can say that it could be related to what is written in a person's palm (based on the interpretation of the palmist or expert), but then again no one can prove it. For me, it's not really a question of whether it works or not. It's more of, if the person believes it or not, which is why keeping an open mind is crucial especially if you wanted to become a proficient palmist.

What is Palmistry?

Palmistry or Chiromancy is the study and interpretation of the human palms. Palmist or palm readers basically look at the hands of their subjects or customers and perform a thorough analysis of the many aspects of the hand, and from there draws hypothetical meanings in accordance to the rules and structure of palmistry.

There are many factors to consider before one can do a proficient palm reading; usually, experts try to determine first the nature of the person they're trying to read. It involves learning about the subject's character, personality, mentality, physical aspects, sexuality, and background as well as other essential factors such as the complexity and characteristics of the hand and fingers. Every hand is unique, and it tells a different story. Just like fingerprints, you can never find the exact same hand print because every individual who ever lived is quite 'special,' perhaps it is what makes us human. There may be some similarities in terms of patterns but it's not the same. Even if individuals have the exact same hand print, for sure, they still came from different backgrounds and have different set of personalities which will alter the meaning of their palms altogether.

Each pair of hands for one individual is also unique; you don't get the exact same hand print for both your left and right hands, which is why it should also be treated individually. If a palmist says that they can predict when an individual is going to get married and have kids, or when will someone dies they are most likely a fraud or a *charlatan* because they have lost touched with reality and became too idealistic already. A true palmist or a proficient reader should not claim anything; you can quickly tell or gauge if they're proficient or not by the number of years they've been in the field or by how well they assess everything before making any assumptions – not conclusions.

Despite of palmistry's long history, it is still fairly new and still has lots of aspects yet to be discovered. Some experts say that palmistry can be used to treat psychological illnesses or mental issues because the nature of its process involves exploring a person's inner self to reveal one's conflicts and draw 'predictions' from there. It's almost the same with what psychologist or mental therapist do to a patient in order for him/her to get in touch with his/her inner self to resolve underlying issues. Palmistry could be one of the treatments that could help in curing psychiatric illnesses in the future according to some experts.

Time can only tell if palmistry can be proven as a valuable tool in the field of psychiatric medicine, and will one day be part of psychology's future. It's still a long way before that can happen, but like any other things, it can be a possibility. Nevertheless, if you are interested in delving into the unknown, and grapple with human nature's complexities then palmistry can help you get started.

How to Distinguish Palm Readers from Frauds

There is a huge difference in knowing something and applying what you know. Dealing with your subject is of utmost importance which is why the application of practical knowledge about every aspect relating to palmistry should be considered because it will benefit you especially when your subject or customer asks questions or make queries about the difference between what you said in your previous readings to your present readings.

Customers especially those who may not entirely believe in the practice of palmistry will definitely have doubts about your reading which is why you need to be able to distinguish yourself from frauds or at least know about the different "types" of palm readers so that you can also determine what kind of palmist or reader you wanted to be.

Technical Palm Reader/ Scientific Hand Analyst

Technical palm readers are the kind of palmists that analyzes and consider every aspect of one's hand. Everything they say has a basis and is structured according the 'rules' of palmistry. Technical palm readers may make educated guess or hypothesis from time to time but it is still based on a lot of factors like the hands, fingers, lines, mounts etc. They don't claim anything based only from their intuition or gut – feeling, everything is factored in base from the structure of their work. One way of knowing if a palmist is a technical one is if they can clarify the statements that they gave, and can at least explain or pinpoint on the subject's hand as to how he/she arrived with a particular assumption. They are only classified as technical analysts.

Psychic/ Clairvoyant Palm Reader

Psychics call themselves "palmist," but it does not necessarily mean that they are experts, in fact, they may not know entirely about the science of palmistry. Usually, clairvoyant palm readers use their intuition to make short term predictions; they do this by making a person's palm as the focal point or medium of their abilities to assume their client's immediate future. If for some reason, you have experienced going to a psychic before, and then switched to a technical palm reader, the latter may not be able to tell you or comment on how the former came up with the previous reading simply because they have different methods.

Card Readers

Card readers foretell a person's future by using tarot cards. The process is simple; they tell clients to shuffle the cards, cut it and deal it out using a number of mystic layouts. Each card has a corresponding meaning but there are also some card readers who combine the standard interpretation with their 'psychic' or intuitive abilities to predict their client's future. According to most experts, tarot card readers often make short term predictions that can be purely incidental to the subject's life. If they already have a general background of a person, they can easily predict their client's future solely based on the overall course of his/her life. Sometimes card readers or psychics do that so that the customers will come back to them after a few months to follow up on their readings, which in turn, could be a lucrative business for them.

Charlatan

Charlatans fall into the category of 'pretenders,' these people often just set themselves up as palmists, they are smooth talkers and basically are good in deception or the art of making people believe in something. They take advantage of people's lack of knowledge, and signs of anxiety to foretell the future. Charlatans are skilled with words, and they are usually charming, often times filled with confidence that they can see and tell what the future holds. Over the years, charlatans accumulated subtle 'pyschic' tricks to put their client at a disadvantage, and also convince them to come back for more. Beware of these fake palm readers because the only basis they have is their overconfident mouths.

A Brief History of Palmistry

There was a time that palmistry or chiromancy was regarded as the demon by itself. Fortunately, in our modern time today it is regarded as an art and a fun hobby. It is even considered now as an interesting field of study especially for those who are the mystical type. Let's take a look at what went down in history, and how the art of palm reading has stood the test of time.

Ancient Civilization

Palm reading dates back to the first human civilization. There were a lot of hand paintings found in prehistoric caves during the Stone Age. The art of palm reading were also found in Vedic scripts, Vedic bible and also early Semitic writings. Aristotle even suggested that there's a connection in the long lines of palm with the gods. During the time of ancient Greeks and Romans, palmistry is actually regarded as a precise science. Prominent figures such as Hypocrites, Galen and Julius Caesar, philosophers, and even warriors have been learning it as if it was an important field of study – which it was, back then. Many scholars and religious personalities debated the academic nature of palmistry which actually ended in a positive note because many guides were published about palmistry line reading, however, because of the rise of Christianity, palmistry and other practices similar to it has been viewed as heresy because it lacks factual basis and it is simply not a 'sound' concept.

Medieval Era

During medieval times, the art of palm reading was restricted by the church because many religious people viewed it as "black magic," after all no one but God can truly tell what the future holds. However, there are still some people who risked doing the practice that they ended up being tortured to their deaths. During the medieval times, the people who practice palm reading are regarded as 'wizards.' Palmistry is proclaimed as witchcraft and a tool of the devil, and again the people who practice it were thrown off a cliff and killed in agony. However, because of the tough handling for this practice, many people over the years have been curious and became more open minded about palm line readings. The practice eventually gained popularity and amazingly survived to this day.

Present Day Palmistry

As years went by, church laws surrounding chiromancy has subsided as the world becomes more open than ever to different concepts and various ideologies. Palmistry and all its basic readings have been passed on from one generation to another, it gained popularity in many countries, and it even became a fair profession for some. Sometimes people study it just for fun or as a hobby, while some believers are so open that they connect everything that happens in their life or in their future to what the lines of their palms have indicated. Whether or not you believe in the art of palm reading, I think all of us can agree that it is an interesting topic to study and learn about.

Chapter Two: Palm Reading Proficiency

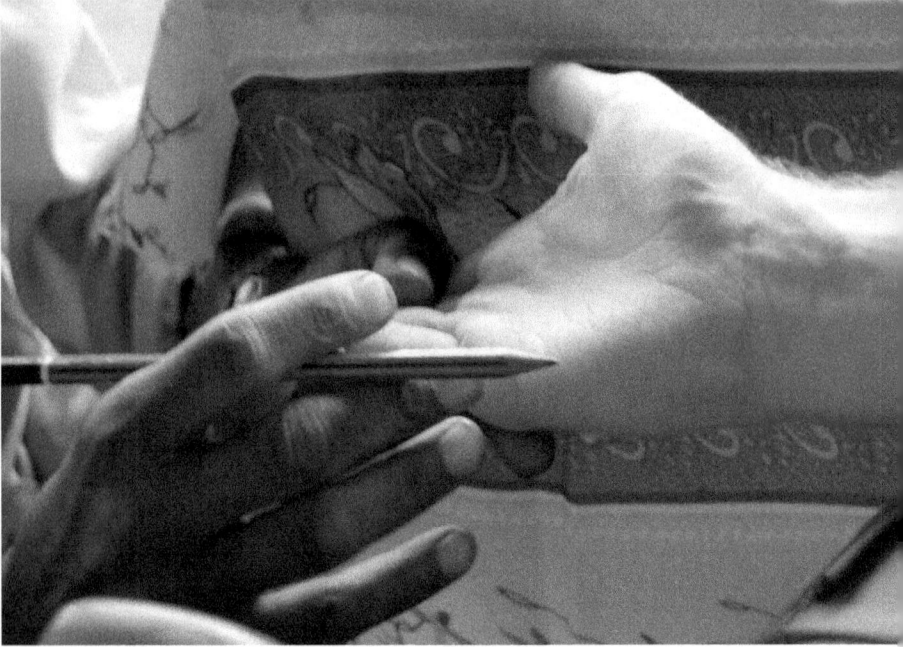

The first step in attaining palm reading proficiency after having an open mindset is to learn the basics of the system by heart. Palm experts don't just memorize the "rules" and corresponding meaning of the lines, they analyze it, weigh in all the factors involve, and work around palmistry's set of structure or process before making any predictions.

If you want to be a proficient hand reader, you have to continuously evolve as a palmist by constantly refining your skills, and developing your own 'style of reading' in accordance with the art. It's the same as learning a new language, you don't just learn the basics of the words or the meaning behind it, you also need to know how to use it in a sentence, how to speak/write properly in accordance with the rules of grammar, but still have the ability to bend it on your own sense of speaking/ writing style, and be able to express your feelings through the medium as how it means to you while keeping in mind the person you're talking to.

Just like language or any other fields of study, many factors should be considered before making any conclusions, claims or in this case, predictions. Time is of the essence, you'll get better at reading palms by practicing it over a period of time and learning from the craft over and over again. In this chapter, you'll be provided with information and some tips that can help you in becoming a proficient palm reader (or at least close to being one).

Can the Hand Really Foretell the Future?

Before giving you some tips on how to become proficient in palm reading, there's one issue that needs to be address first before anyone can actually believe that he/she could have the capability of diagnosing a person's hand and have a 'glimpse' of someone's future.

Many people doubt whether or not a person can actually learn the skill of reading palms. The whole question of someone predicting the future or even having a sneak peek of it is a highly controversial topic – one that has been debated and argued about over the course of human history!

There are people who believe that the hand can foretell the future but obviously, most people think that it's an outrageous idea, and most refuse to consider the possibility. The surprising fact is that all of us can actually foretell the future! In fact, we are doing it in our everyday lives. An example is setting up a schedule or following a timetable, you are predicting exactly what will happen or what you want to happen on your day with accuracy – that in itself already makes you a "fortune teller."

Another example is in the field of medicine, a doctor can usually tell if his/her patient has a fatal form of disease, how long will he/she recover, or if the patient is likely to die or not. If you think about it, there's no book or rules that specifically tell physicians on how to make such claims (about when a person will die if he/she acquired a certain kind of illness in a certain way etc.). A doctor's diagnosis is base from facts and scientific structure but it is still not definite, circumstances can change, therefore they cannot say exactly what will happen, but the question is how come doctors 'predict' their patient's 'fate' with a reasonable degree of accuracy more often than not?

The reason for this is simple, doctors know how a certain disease works by heart and through their many years of experience; they know the facts, the effects, how the disease will progress, and every single factor that needs to be considered – not to mention the many guides and 'clues' in the form of symptoms or lab tests as well as the patient's history. They draw conclusions from these factors; they can gauge the patient's fate and predict the likely outcome by connecting the dots based from such factors, the overall structure of science and their many years of experience. And so it is with palmistry – the only difference is that palmistry is dealing with the psychology or essence of the human brain and an individual's inner self.

Nothing can be more complex than the human brain, there are still lots of things to discover about how it works, but it seems like scientists are still far from learning the whole truth about it because it's constantly evolving.

According to experts, the hand is the servant of the brain, which is why consequently it is the place where the brain "prints out" its expectations. Basically the brain anticipates the future trend of a person's life by acquiring all the existential and non – existential knowledge as well as an individual's surroundings over a period of time. It records everything, creates patterns, and connects possible outcomes. It then makes a conclusion off of that and print out its expectations or predictions in the hands.

Most people argue and negate the predictive value of palmistry because lines of the hands are known to change sometimes. It is true that hand prints can change but it is a very unusual occurrence. However, if it does, it can only mean that the person is undergoing a change in their inner nature which was not previously anticipated by the brain. It's something so different that no record of it can be found from the person's life archives. Therefore the brain cannot make any substantial conclusion off of it but it is aware of the change and the reaction to a certain event or new occurrence. From there, the brain creates modification in its inputs which is then reflected by the change of lines on the hand.

As a student of palmistry, it's very important for you to know that dealing with your subject's future life through reading a mark on his/her hand is not a guarantee because everything can always change. You're basically just interpreting or translating what their own brains predicted – you don't make the prediction, your subject's brain does. You are just reading them but you also have to explain that their brain's print out is just something that the mind concluded based on past occurrences, therefore it could be different from what can actually happen in their present or future reality. The mark or the hand print only indicates what the mind anticipates for the future but there's always a possibility that something unlikely can occur which could bring forth the modification or change in the person's life not expected by the brain. Just like how doctors gauge their patient's conditions, or how stock brokers predict the highs and lows of the market, palmistry does the same thing and follows the same logic based from previous occurrences.

So can the hand foretell the future? Yes – but not exactly. The person's present choices can alter future events, something that even an individual's own brain cannot predict. Remember that the future is not yet written, it's only anticipated. Do yourself a favor, surprise your mind!

How to Become a Proficient Palm Reader

Usually, people seek clarity or help from palmists because they are worried about some things in their life – some very important matters so to speak. Often times, people wanted a simple yes or no answer from palm readers. However, as what you've been learning so far, it's not as easy as you think, and there is no straightforward answer when it comes to chiromancy. If you are studying or have been practicing the art and science of palm reading, people will usually ask impossible questions such as who are they going to marry, or what should they do about a particular situation they are in. If you are serious about becoming a palmist, you should never rush, you must stay in control of your readings and don't just read people's palms because you feel the need of answering their questions.

There is no quick routine – type of palm reading, as mentioned before, every person is different, and circumstances are always changing which is why every reading has the possibility to be altered. If they ask you such questions, don't give your subjects a ready – made prediction because it will not benefit both of you either way. You'll have trouble defending yourself in the long run if in case your subjects have a follow – up question. As a palmist, you have to know the basic idea of palmistry's important points, and you should have a method that will enable you to work through your subject's palms based in a constructive manner so you can read them objectively.

Like any other things, learning takes time, and the quickest way to refine your skill is to take things step by step so that you can get better at it. You will develop greater depth and accuracy as you increase your knowledge, and practice it over time. A true palmist is never afraid to admit that chiromancy also has limitations; don't be afraid to ask questions (similar to a psychiatrist or a therapist) because through this method you can learn more about the person's past events which could help you understand your subject and also enhance your ability to understand various aspects and markings in hand prints.

Keep in mind that palm readers should not "blind their customers with science." According to Benham, a famous palmistry author, he said that some insecure palmists or dishonest palm readers sometimes use scientific terms or jargons so that their subjects will have trouble understanding or will not further ask questions from them. The whole purpose of palm reading is to read and interpret palms to help people gain a better understanding of themselves. Therefore, you should be able to say your interpretations in lay man's term; you should choose your words in a way that will enable your subject to make sense of your readings.

If you want to be proficient in palm reading, and gain trust from your subjects, you should be able to practice the value of honesty. This is the most important value that palmists or practitioners should possess right from the start. It will not only help you become proficient, but it will also keep you grounded and not take advantage of people's innocence or lack of knowledge. Don't let yourself be tempted in saying something just to make your customers feel better, don't be afraid to tell the truth, and admit it to your subject/s if you really don't know the answer to all their questions.

Chapter Three: Cheirology
The Basics of Palmistry

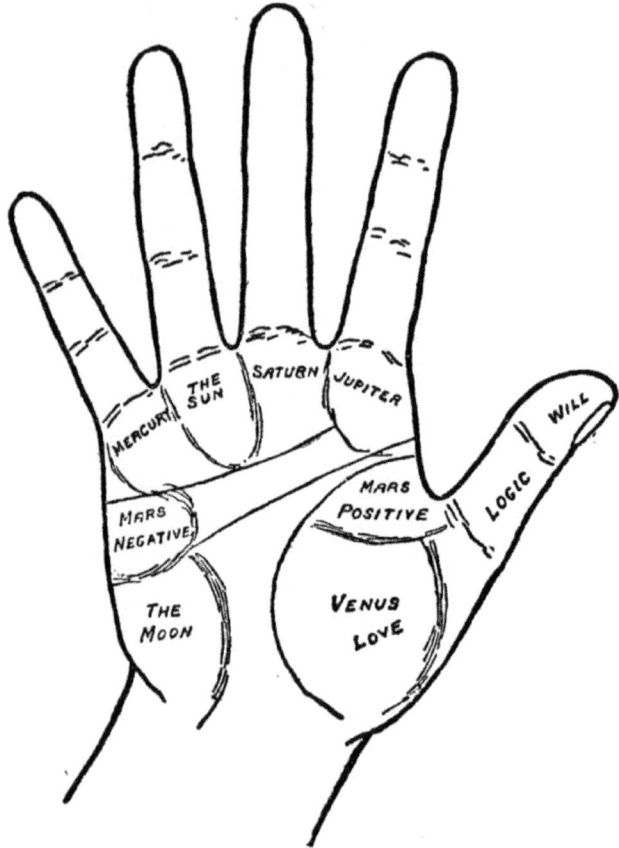

In this chapter you will learn about Cheirology or the study of the physical aspects of the hand. As mentioned in the previous chapter, the hands are the "servant of the brain," our hands are involved in almost everything we do in our everyday lives. Before we get to the basics of palm reading, a student or practitioner should also study and familiarize every aspect of the hand because it is also part of the "bigger picture."

You must learn how to deal with various factors because it affects how you interpret and read the meaning behind the hand prints.

What is Cheirology?

Cheirology has very little to do with the lines in the palms, however it is necessary to understand the anatomy of the hand your reading for you to have a more in – depth conclusion and give a more accurate interpretation of your subject's hand print. Cheirology involves the study of the hand itself (both left and right) including the length of the fingers, its nails, the fingertips, the 'mounts' found in the palm, the texture, color, size and even its firmness or softness.

Most people who are trying to study palmistry for the first time are so keen to only focus on the lines and hand prints; they fail to pay attention to other parts of the hand that also contributes to the accuracy of the readings and in fact, part of the whole palm reading process. The study of the hands (fingers, size, length etc.) is key to understanding the nature and character of your customer or subject.

For some beginners, certain issues like the length of the fingers or size of the hands causes a lot of confusion. It is quite hard to classify if the fingers are long, medium or short and what type of hand your subject possess. (Later on we'll tackle the different types of hands as well as the significance and meaning behind the sizes, color, texture etc.) This is where you should a sense of balance and use of your own judgment comes in. Your intuitiveness can only be developed through years of experience and constant use. However, you can still classify fingers or hands properly as long as you balance everything out; one option will stand out more than the other option but make sure to assess it thoroughly so you can make the right call. Classifying the type of hand or length/type of fingers properly is crucial because it has significance in the overall reading. Only time and practice can make a palmist develop a good eye for quickly assessing and classifying the hand appropriately.

In the next section, you'll be given a list of the different parts of the hand involved, and how it helps in accurately reading your subject's hand print.

Physical Aspects of the Hand

Before getting to the basics of palm reading, here's a brief outline of the factors that you're going to have to deal with to aid you in reading hand prints accurately. In the next few chapters, we will delve more into how these factors affect the overall meaning of your subject's palm for you to see the significance and intricacy of the details.

Skin Texture

Skin texture in palmistry refers to the innate degree of refinement. You can gauge one's skin texture by looking at the back of your subject's hand. You will need to determine the texture of the person you're reading to be able to give an accurate interpretation.

Palm Color

Determining the palm color will indicate the vitality and warmth of your subject.

Hand Consistency

The consistency of the hand indicates the energy level of your customer. You can determine the 'fullness' or 'nothingness' of life of the person you're reading through feeling his/her hand and noting the degree of its elasticity or the ability of the body to recover its shape after being deformed. If the hand has a springiness quality to it, it is elastic.

Hand Flexibility

This may be hard to fathom especially for beginners. Having a flexible hand usually indicates the degree of mental flexibility of an individual as well as its adaptability to be open to new ideas and circumstances.

Fingers Lengths

The length of a person's finger usually indicates the degree of thought that your customer is likely to give in a particular matter, or how deep they delve into a certain subject that attracts their attention.

Finger Knots

The finger knots indicate the thinking process of an individual. It's either a cover smooth type or knotty fingers.

Finger Phalanges

The finger phalanges deal with a person's mind and a particular matter that he/she is most concerned with. It could be his/her family life, her marriage, her relationships, her career etc.

Fingertip Shapes

The shape of a person's fingertip is an indicator of a person's mental outlook.

The Thumb

Thumbs are classified into different types just like the size of the hand and the fingers. Studying the thumb will make a palmist get a clear insight of his/her subject's character or personality.

The Mounts

The mounts (which will be discussed later in this book) will enable a palmist to determine your subject's deepest desires, their passion and what they truly want in life.

Active and Passive Zones in the Hand

This will help a palmist understand if the subject likes to make things happen or just let circumstances happen to them.

Left and Right Hands

The first you need to determine before reading a palm is if your subject is left or right handed. After which you have to examine both hands before making any conclusions or determining which hand you will settle with to perform a reading.

The standard meaning of the two hands is that the "active hand" or the hand that does most of the work is the part that records the present, while the "passive hand" usually records the qualities the subject was born with – or who you are by default, you can say that this is an individual's baseline before the brain made assumptions about the person's future. Most people are right handed (active hand), while the left hand is the passive one; for left handed people, it's just vice – versa.

However, if that is the case then the passive hand is unlikely to change since it's something that you are born with, so it's probably better to say that the passive hand indicates qualities and an individual's disposition after he/she finished laying out the foundations of his/her life.

Most psychologists agree that it is during our childhood where we lay life's foundation to aid us as we grow old. The decisions, choices, conclusions, assumptions we made during our formative years affects how we will live as adults, this includes how we deal with other people and our inner self as well as how we look at the world where we live. These are the basis of the person we will eventually become, thus the difference of the two hands – the passive hand indicates subconscious levels of who we were when our biological system changed as we go from one phase to another, while the active hand indicates the outer and more conscious selves, and how a person have develop and evolved from that point.

Comparing both hands will determine your subject's progression and development over the years, whether they developed in a positive or negative way. If the prints of both hands are somewhat similar, then it could be an indication that an individual just sort of went with the flow with whatever disposition or talent they were given when their childhood was over.

If the active hand shows negative prints than the passive hand, it indicates that they fell to the many temptations given before them, and perhaps failed to make use of their talents and capabilities after their childhood stage. If the active hand shows more positive prints than the passive one, then that means that an individual made an effort to enhance his/her given talent and build something from whatever they started during their youth. Sometimes this development came about because of necessity but other times it is a person's own choice.

A change in the formation of hand prints are very rare, but if ever you come across with something like that, it only goes to show that drastic changes have been made by that person particularly his/her inner being and subconscious as well the foundation laid during his/her childhood. It is also most likely that the person also altered the values or ideas he/she had cherished ever since. This could likely happen if the person underwent a very traumatic event that led him/her to change his/her core values and foundation.

Texture of the Skin

The first ever step in becoming a palm reader is to check the quality of your subject's skin. In this book, the texture will be divided into seven groups: extremely – fine, fine, medium – fine, medium, medium – coarse, coarse, and extremely coarse. So that beginners can easily grasp the concept and also be able to classify the texture of the palms that one will encounter. Assessing the texture of your skin is essential to learn about your subject's natural degree of innate personality.

Basically, the finer the texture the more sophisticated a person is. It means that they are more sensitive, and their attitude or feelings can be easily disturbed by something that emotionally upsets them. If the person has a rougher and coarser skin texture that usually indicates that he/she is more basic, and down – to – earth kind of person. These kinds of people are simple and can't be affected easily by circumstances that happen to them.

In the next section you'll be given a quick and easy to read overview of each skin texture so you can easily classify the kind of hand your reading.

Extremely – Fine Skin Texture

- These kinds of hand texture are extremely rare.
- Aside from being fine, it is also very soft and delicate which indicates that they are very sophisticated in nature, and they get easily upset when a situation offends their inner sense or refinement.
- These people tend to love fine or delicate things and dislike anything that is vulgar or brutal because it could somehow cause them pain.

Fine Skin Texture

- This is one of the most common skin textures you will encounter. It's almost the same with extremely – fine texture.
- These kinds of people like to hang – out with equally sophisticated people.
- They tend to respect more down – to – earth people like those who are in entry – level jobs or something

similar but they may not find it easy or enjoy their company in a social situation.

Medium – Fine Skin Texture

- It indicates your subject is well balanced in their attitude between that which is down – to – earth and that which is refined or sophisticated person.
- Since it is still classified as medium – fine these kinds of people is still refined in nature.

Medium Skin Texture

- These kinds of palms are also rare, not a lot of experts use this kind of classification.
- It can be hard to identify but medium skin texture has certain elasticity to it.
- People who possess a medium skin texture often strike a balance between sophistication and basic.

Medium - Coarse Skin Texture

- Easily recognizable and could be encountered frequently.
- Even if there's a certain sense of coarseness to it, it still isn't coarse enough to be classified as rough.
- Usually indicates being well – balanced but has an inclination towards earthiness.

Coarse Skin Texture

- Usually recognizable because the skin on the back of the hand looks rough and leathery and indicates a person who is inclined to be simple, uncomplicated and also down – to – earth nature
- These kinds of people are usually not interested in the subtleties of life, and have a strong dislike for anything they see as being pretentious.

Extremely Coarse Skin Texture

- Also very rare to find, similar to extremely fine texture.
- It is easily recognizable as the skin on the back of the hand looks very rough and coarse looks like extremely low grade leather.
- It is usually found on the kinds of people that have primitive lifestyles.
- People with this texture are primitive in their innate nature and also indifferent to any form of sophistication or what they consider as pretentious.
- These kinds of people are so uncomplicated, very simple and cannot understand the complexities of modern society; perhaps they are also very practical.

Hand Consistency

The consistency of the hand along with skin texture, palm color and flexibility can help any practitioner read the palms better because it gives a huge amount of information. In fact, according to many experts even if you have limited knowledge of palmistry and you can only rely on skin texture, consistency, flexibility, and color, you can still be capable of doing accurate and in-depth readings! This is how important these factors are!

Hand consistency is determined by taking your subject's hand and then exerting a gentle pressure to see how elastic the flesh is. Try shaking their hand for you to get the idea. You should also get your subject to stretch out their hand and try pressing into the flesh of the palm with the ball of your thumb to see how much resistance there is.

Just like the skin texture, hand consistency can be classified to many types namely; very hard, hard, elastic-hard, elastic, elastic-soft, soft, and very soft and flabby. In the next section you'll be given a quick and easy to read overview of each types of hand consistency so you can easily classify your subject's hand.

Very Hard Hands

- Very rare to find, and certainly has extreme indications
- Virtually has no elasticity, and can be hard to press or squeeze
- Usually indicates that your subject is a very energetic person, extremely active and always ready to do anything he/she could possibly do.
- These kinds of people lack intelligence and often times they could be working at something without giving any real thought.

Hard Hands

- Frequently found compared to very hard hands category. Also quite recognizable because you can squeeze their hand or press it but there's just little give to it. However, there's a sign of elasticity
- Almost has similar traits with very hard hands, the only difference perhaps is that they are not quite as mindless in the way they spend their energy.

Elastic Hard Hands

- Has the kind of hand that has a degree of elasticity enough to prevent it from being classified as hard.
- Usually indicate that your subject is full of energy but it is intelligently directed.

Elastic Hands

- Has a certain firmness and quite difficult to press but once you let go the flesh bounces back like a rubber ball.
- Usually indicates that the person also has a huge amount of energy but also intelligent in the way they do things.
- They work hard and they work smart; keeping in mind what they're doing and don't want to waste their energy into something useless.
- They are also full of life but they're quite balance
- Usually found in successful people.

Elastic Soft Hands

- Even if the hands are elastic, you can easily recognize or differentiate it because there is certain softness to the flesh, it doesn't bounce back like the elastic hands.
- Usually, it indicates that a person is willing to work very hard to get what they want. They are the kind of people that have a sense of laziness but their sometimes it overrides their desire to work.
- It also goes to show that the person enjoys working as much as they enjoy other pleasures.

- They tend to seek a job that can be enjoyable but not too mentally or physically demanding.

Soft Hands

- Very recognizable because it is very soft once pressed and lacks elasticity
- Usually indicates that a person is lazy and likes to indulge on certain things too much.
- Usually has all the skill and intelligence but lacks effort.

Very Soft and Flabby Hands

- These are extreme indications and also very recognizable because once you squeeze the hand it looks like their flesh want to ooze out!
- Also a high indicator that the person is very lazy
- More of a dreamer and not a doer
- Don't usually make an effort to materialize their ideas or dreams.

Hand Flexibility

The flexibility of the hand indicates the versatility of your subject's mind and their ability to adapt their mentality to new and progressive ideas, new ways of doing things, and changing circumstances.

The rule of thumb for flexibility is that the more flexible the hand, the more flexible the mentality. The stiffer the hand, the stiffer, more rigid, and more unbending the mentality. To gauge the degree of flexibility you should hold the tips of your subject's fingers in one hand support the wrist with the other and then exert a gentle pressure until you have bent the hand back as far as it will go. Be careful not to hurt your subject!

Palm Color

Palm colors can provide a reader about the temperament of their subject whether they are warm/genial, hot – blooded or can't control their temper, cold – selfish or self – contained. However, various factors such as the room temperature as well as the country of origin also matters, make sure to take everything into consideration before saying any statements. Colors are also divided into several groups namely: very red, red, pinky-red, pink, pinky-white, white, and very white.

In the next section you'll be given a quick and easy to read overview of each palm colors so you can easily classify your subject's hand.

Very – Red Color

- Usually indicates an extreme or an intense temper, and also quite excessive.
- Generally doesn't exercise moderation; so if for example they are alcoholics, it'll be difficult for them to stop

Red Color

- Can be frequently found; also shows quite an intense and ardent temper
- When red palmed people fall in love, they love passionately but sometimes their devotion tends to frighten their lovers away.

Pinky – Red Color

- Red is heat and pink is warmth. If your subject has a pinky – red palms then that means they are warm people but are also inclined to being intense from time to time.

Pink Color

- Pink palms are the finest color or say the ideal color, if your subject has pinking palms then that means he/she warm, cheerful, bright and animated in a way.

- They are congenial companions and exude just the right amount of warmth in their personality.

Pinky - White Color

- Also easily recognizable because it's a mix of pinking and whitish color
- Usually indicates that the person is warm in nature but they tend to be "cool" about things.
- They are warm and also cheerful but can be inclined to having a lukewarm attitude.

White Color

- White is equivalent with being "cold," that means the person lack warmth and is usually self – contained.
- Their minds are usually active but they don't have a burning desire to seek out other people
- Generally selfish and are not helpful in nature.

Extremely - White Color

- Very rare to find just like an extremely – red colored palm. Often appears as pallid and the palm looks lifeless.
- They have a cold outlook and attitude towards life, very self – contained/ selfish, mystical and completely lack compassion.

- When they fall in love even with their ideal partner, they don't show or express themselves, and usually more idealistic than passionate.

Yellow and Blue Colored Palms

Yellow colored palms usually indicates a moody type of personality and is quite pessimistic, on the other hand, blue colored palms usually indicates a sluggish blood circulation and often times has a weak heart (both physically and emotionally).

Types of Fingers, Palms, and Mount

For you to gain more insight about the true character of the person you're reading, you also have to consider factors such as the shape of the palms, the shape and length of the fingers, the fingertips, the nails, the thumb as well as the so – called mounts before you can actually proceed in reading the lines. Doing so will give you a more accurate reading and will also enhance your ability as a palmist. Once you learn all these essentials, you'll be able to read easier and in a constructive manner.

Finger Length

After considering other factors like the skin texture, hand consistency, flexibility, and palm colors, the next thing to classify is the length of the fingers. The length will give you an insight about the degree of your subject's mentality. In the next section you'll be given a quick and easy to read of the different finger lengths so you can easily classify your subject's hand.

Very Long Fingers

- Like other extremes, very long finger types are rarely found.
- This kind of people has overdeveloped mentality or the kinds of person who thinks about everything.
- These kinds of people are usually mentally engrossed in their subject matter that not even a single detail escapes their attention.
- They often lose sight of the "bigger picture."

Long Fingers

- Quite common
- Usually indicates that the person thinks a great deal about everything that attracts their attention.
- They are very sensitive and also prone to being suspicious of others.

Medium - Long Fingers

- It is relatively long but still not long enough to be classified as long fingers.
- Usually indicates a good balance between a desire to think about things and pay attention to details, and they want to get things done.

Medium Fingers

- Usually indicates a balanced mental approach
- These kinds of people give enough mental attention to whatever they are concentrating on, but no more than enough.
- They deal with all the necessary details and then concentrate on getting it done.

Medium - Short Fingers

- Also shows that the person is well balanced in the use of their mentality.
- Usually have a desire to take an overall view of things and avoid details they consider unimportant.

Short Fingers

- Usually indicates a person who doesn't like to deal with unnecessary details.
- Most of the time, these kinds of people just like to get to the point.
- They are quick in making decisions and because of that they plan things on a large scale which can be a disadvantage at times because they tend to overlook important details that can cause problems.

Very - Short Fingers

- Usually indicates that a person also dislikes thinking about e-v-e-r-y thing (this kind of people should not get into jobs like event planning or something similar).
- They are also motivated by their instincts and also wants to get things done quickly.

Types of Fingertips

The shapes of the fingers represent your subject's mind, while its fingertips indicate your subject's mental outlook. In this section you'll be given a quick and easy to read about the meaning and indications of the different six types of fingers/fingertips namely; spatulate, square, rounded, conic, philosophic and psychic.

Spatulate Fingers

- If your subject's fingertips are flare out or broad in its tips like a chemist's spatula, then you can classify it as a spatulate finger.
- Usually indicates that your subject is very active and someone who refuses to be conventional or accept things as they are.
- These kinds of people are always looking for something new or different. They're the kind of people that don't follow the status quo; just because everyone else does something in a certain way, is no reason why they should do the same.
- Usually there are the adventure – type, explorers and trail blazers in the industry. They always try to be original, disruptive and love to "break the rules."
- A person who is very innovative and possess a great deal of energy to achieve something.

Square Fingers

- Well, you can easily identify it if the fingertips are square – shaped.
- Usually indicates that the person is punctual, practical, organize and systematic in everything they do.

- Quite conservative in a way that they strictly follow a schedule or routine.
- These kinds of people don't like to break away from tradition or the status quo.

Conic Fingers

- Also common and recognizable; the fingers from base to tip give the appearance of a cone hence the name.
- Usually indicates that your subject is impulsive, unrealistic, emotional, and easily influenced by their current mood.
- Their mental outlook is both receptive and impractical and they find that having to do things in an orderly manner is boring.
- Idealistic in their outlook, they live for the moment, love to the company of other, and just want to enjoy life.
- These kinds of people have an artistic temperament (where beauty is more important than practicality), however, because they lack regularity they don't often accomplish many things.

Round Fingers

- Very common and is a combination of square and conic shapes.

- Indicates that your subject is practical in their mental outlook, and are not tied down by a need for absolute system and regularity.
- Slight rounding of the tips indicates that their practical outlook is sometimes tempered by idealism and intuition.

Psychic or Pointed - Tip Fingers

- Very rare to find; the fingers are very long and pointed, shaped like a long conic finger.
- The pointedness usually indicates that a person shows great inspiration, idealism, and a very impractical or unrealistic outlook on life.
- Since the fingers are long, it means that the mental world is dominant but usually has a sensitive feeling. They are always suspicious, doubtful of others and gets offended easily.

Philosophic Fingers

- This kind of finger is a combination of long fingers, pointed tips, and knotty joints.
- The long fingers indicates a developed mental world, the pointed tips shows an idealistic outlook while the knots indicates that the person has a habit of analyzing everything.
- Overall, people with this finger shapes love reasoning, and are also analytic. Sometimes they are

also idealistic especially to topics like philosophy, theology, and the meaning of life.

- Also has a habit of analyzing their ideals and inspirations.

Types of Finger Knots

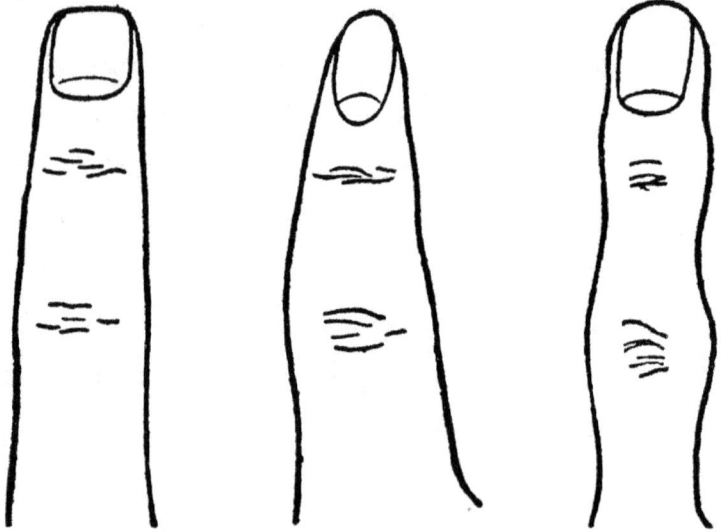

THE SQUARE WITH
SMOOTH JOINTS

THE POINTED

THE KNOTTY

Finger knots have two types – smooth or knotty, you can determine it by noticing how developed a person's knuckle joint is.

Knotty Fingers

People with knotty fingers indicate that a person has a powerful or strong mental world. It usually means that your subject is thoughtful, careful, precise, analyzes his/her move and they are also organize in their life.

They're the kind of people who think about a matter first, before accepting anything. They must first analyze it, and examine it from every point of view before agreeing or getting them to agree on something. They wish to get to the facts and to the bottom of any subject and they don't want be rushed but once they have made up their mind on something they will never swerve from their opinion.

The top joints are called the "knots of mental order," if your subject's joints are developed, it means that he/she is someone who tends to reason out everything that is of a mental nature. They take nothing for granted and examine every point, and every perspective. They then file it away in their precise and well-ordered brain.

The middle joints are referred to as the "knots of material order," if your subject's joints are developed, it means that he/she tends to organize all the material aspects of their life. In their home and place of work everything will be neat, in order, and put away in a place where it can be easily found.

Smooth Fingers

Smooth fingers indicate that your subject is someone who thinks quickly and intuitively. As previously mentioned knotty fingers show that the mind is restricted because it analyzes too much, smooth fingers shows that the mind does not stop to analyze everything which is why they tend to decide on things much quickly. Smooth-fingered people are quite artsy, they appreciate beauty and they are also spontaneous in their nature. They think quickly and often make decisions based on impulse or intuition, something a knotty-fingered person would never do. Unfortunately, they are also the kind of people who take a lot of things for granted because it will get them through their day's work faster and easier.

Smooth fingers also develop knots, and even if your subject gives reasons (because of sports, work etc.) as to why their hands have developed knots, it only develops as the result of a psychological change within the individual.

For instance, as people grow older or become more matured, they tend to develop a more analytical outlook, which is why the fingers will become more developed or knotty. Although this is the case, it doesn't mean that smooth-fingered people don't analyze things, the difference is that they only analyze things that they think are important whereas knotty – fingered people tend to overthink every single thing about a matter.

Types of Finger Phalanges

If the fingers represent the mind, the phalanges of the fingers represent the world within the mind. These are the physical, practical and mental.

If the bottom phalanges on all the fingers of your subject are long then that means that his/her mind is limited by matters that relates to their physical and personal self. When they think about things, they think about their home, pleasure, and personal comforts.

If the middle phalanges are longest, it means that the mind concentrates mostly on matters of a practical nature which commonly relates to the outside world in some way.

If the top phalanges are longest it means that your subject's mind is very taken up with matters of a mental or intellectual nature.

For reading purposes finger phalanges can only be accurate when there are clear differences in their various lengths. If one phalanx is only slightly more developed than another it means that the mind is only slightly more inclined to concentrate on the aspects indicated by the longer or thicker phalanx.

If the bottom phalanges are not just long, but also fat and puffy, then your subject is someone who is sensually indulgent as their mind is almost obsessed with matters regarding their physical and personal pleasure.

If the bottom phalanges are long, and narrow that means that your subject are choosy with what they eat and the type of pleasures they will want to indulge in.

Type of Nails

If your subject has a long and narrow nail it indicates that he/she is mental or idealistic by nature. It also means that they simply lack robustness and you may not see them doing heavy manual labor, participating in strenuous sporting events or doing things that require much effort. Broad nails, on the other hand indicate a robust constitution.

Short nails are generally broad and besides showing a robust constitution. They're the kind of people that tends to be argumentative and something of a fault picker.

If your subject's nail is very short and very broad, it means that they are extremely critical. They're the kind of people that even if they know they are in the wrong, they are still willing to argue for the sake of arguing.

Nail Color

As always pink is a good sign to find because it indicates good health. Blue shows a sluggish circulation which may be due to a weak heart, while a purple nail shows that some form of heart difficulty is likely, especially if there are patches of blue in the palm. Nails that have little white spots mean that the nervous system is currently under a lot of strain.

Fluted Nails

Fluted nails usually indicate a tense or nervous disposition. The greater the degree of fluting, the greater the degree of nervous tension and in an extreme situation, the nails becomes white and brittle. An extremely fluted nails curve slightly down to protect the finger tips, and also curves upwards in an arch. It shows an extreme degree of nervous disorder and often season on people who recently suffered a stroke or some other form of nervous illness.

Types of Palms

There are three different types of palms namely; square palms, spatulate palms and conic palms. Other books may have more classifications, however, it all still falls in these three major types. In the next section you'll be given a quick and easy to read of the different shapes of the palm so you can easily classify your subject's hand and gain more insight.

Square Palms

- If your subject has square palms, it usually means that they are practical by nature, even if you'll see a conic finger that shows their idealistic or impulsive mental outlook feature, they are still pretty much the realistic type.
- If you encounter a sort of rectangular shaped – palm (which still classifies as square), it indicates that their physical or practical world is not develop.

Spatulate Palms

- Usually indicates that your subject's instinctive nature is original and inclined to be different.
- If it is broader at the base, they will be original and different in the world of ideas because of the

developed Mount of Luna which shows imaginative powers. (more on mounts later)

- If the palm is broader at the top, it means that they are different and original in practical ways.

Conic Palms

- Usually indicates that a person is idealistic and emotional.
- Conic palms usually have a broader base which also indicates that their physical world is well - developed and shows the desire to indulge the physical.
- If your subject has a conic palm but has fine skin texture (refer to skin texture section), then that means they are refined in the way they'll do physical things.

The Thumb

Palmists, authors and founders of modern palmistry agree that the thumb, although part of the fingers, is very important to completely understand your subject because it individualizes a person. As what you've just learned, other aspects of the hands such as the fingertips, palm shapes, finger lengths etc. will give you an insight about your subject's qualities, nature and disposition with regards to their mentality. However, the thumb as what many experts suggest will give you an insight about the person's character or willpower. I'm sure you've heard the saying that a person can have all the talents in the world but if they lack character, talents will be useless to them.

Character or willpower is one of the qualities that distinguish human beings from one another. It's a force that even the almighty cannot predict because it's instinctive and an impulse. In short, character is a choice. You're not actually born with it; you develop your character as you grow old. You make choices based on your belief, your logic reasoning and your core values or from other factors. Anyone can change their character or exercise willpower if they choose to.

In palmistry the thumb can be divided into three sections; the instinctive nature, sentiments, and desires. The second or middle phalanx indicates the powers of logic and reason while the first or top phalanx is the phalanx of will or action. A desire for something (palm) is filtered through logic and reason (second phalanx) before being turned into action and reality (top phalanx).

The Mounts

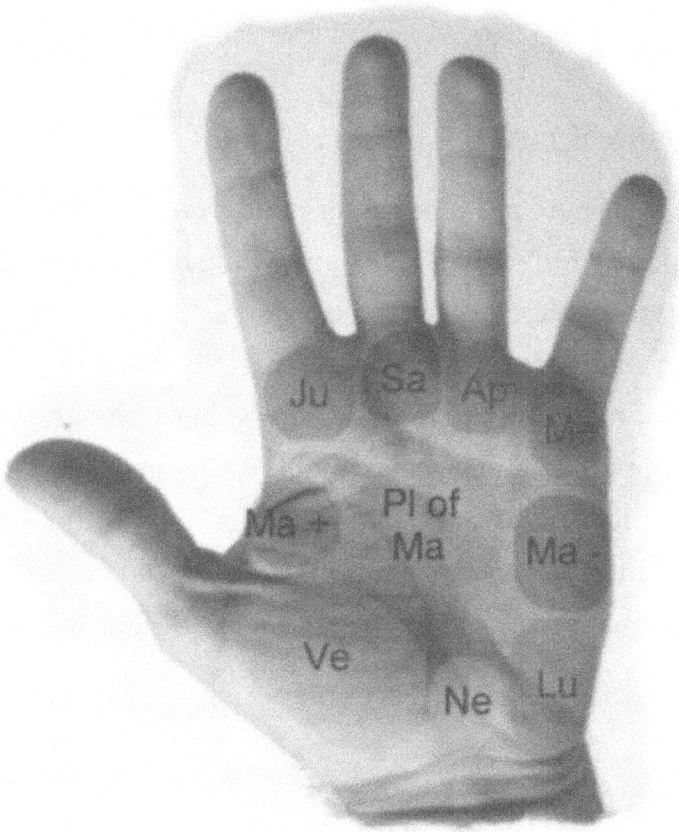

There are seven mounts on the hand namely; Mount of Jupiter, Saturn, Apollo, Mercury, Moon, Venus, and Mount of Mars. Each of which indicates a particular aspect of a subject's nature. The job of the palm reader is to decide on the relative strength of each mount, pick the strongest or most dominating area, and then arrange other mounts into their order of prominence. In this section, you'll be provided with some basic interpretations about each mounts.

It's also recommended that you study the areas of each mounts so that you can be familiar of its locations in the palm.

Mount of Jupiter

There are four fingers underneath each of which is a mount. Under the first or index finger is the Mount of Jupiter which indicates the person's desire to have a control over their life and those who affect it. If the mount of Jupiter is prominent it means that your subject possess a leadership quality. It is an indicator that the person is honest and optimistic. However, if it is flat that means that he/she lacks confidence, and if the mount is over – developed (or really dominant over others) it's an indicator that the person is egoistic and arrogant.

Mount of Saturn

The mount of Saturn is located under the second or middle finger. It indicates a desire for stability and security. It also means that the person is very responsible and seeks wisdom. If the mount is flat, the person could be optimistic and loves to socialize. However, if it is overdeveloped and your subject possess a long finger, it's an indicator that he/she is an introvert or quite distant to people.

Mount of Apollo

It is located under the third or ring finger and usually indicates the desire to express one's own individuality or personal uniqueness. If the mount is well – developed, the person is quite optimistic and warm but if it is flat, it usually means that he/she is cynical and cold.

Mount of Mercury

It is located under the fourth or little finger and usually indicates the desire to communicate. These are the kinds of people who loves to travel and is a go – getter. However, if the mount of Mercury is overdeveloped that indicates the person is a liar. A flat mount means that he/she is often shy and boring.

Mount of Moon or Mount of Luna

Located at the base of the palm across the thumb, if it is well – developed it usually means that the person is compassionate, loving, creative and also enthusiastic about life but if it is flat, it indicates a sense of empathy and also good imagination.

Mount of Venus

Can be found under the thumb, and usually indicates that the degree of generosity and warmness. If it is well – developed it means that they are an interesting companion and leads a social life. If the mount of Venus is overdeveloped it shows that he/she is greedy and wants to acquire material things, and if it is flat that means that your subject lacks passion and he/she is also selfish.

Mount of Mars

The Mount of Mars which is divided into two zones; active and passive; underneath the Mount of Jupiter and inside the Life Line is the Mount of Lower Mars which indicates the person's desire to push or force their way forward in life. Across the hand is the Mount of Upper Mars which indicates their desire to stick to their resolutions and persist in their endeavors.

In the next few chapters, we will delve deeper into the major type of lines in the palm; its indications, significance and proper reading.

Chapter Four: The Line of Heart

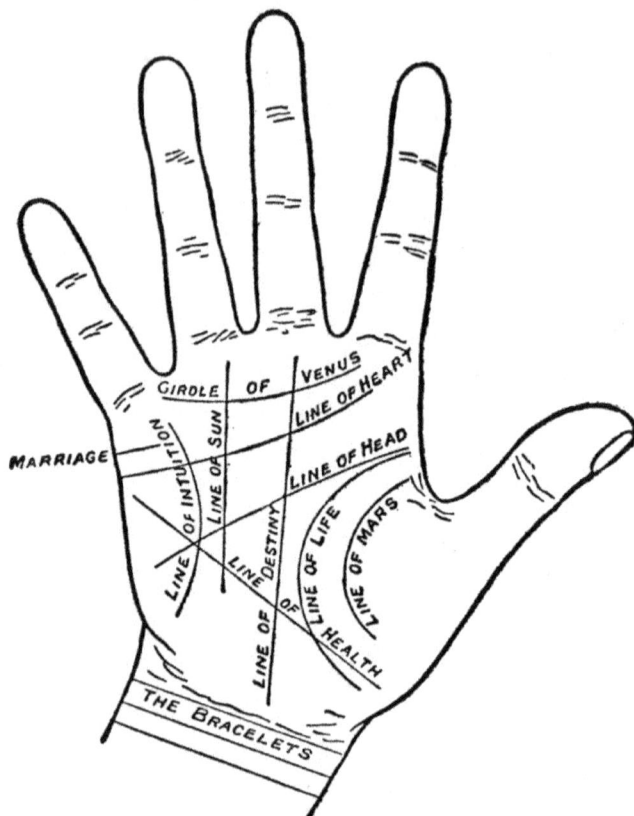

Basically the heart line is all about a person's emotional nature – its depth and also its quality. If the line is clear and long, that means that your subject is governed by their love and affection for their family, friends, relatives, and people in general. The shorter the line, the less influenced they are by their relationships to other people, they are also less inclined to care for others or pay attention to the desires and emotional needs of those who are close to them.

Most people consults a palmist because they wanted to know something about the love life like when they are going to get married, what kind of person they are going to have a relationship with or if it is long – lasting or not. However, it's again not that easy, expert palmists usually restrict themselves with regards to this matter to avoid confusion. They mostly focus on the indications of the heart line that relates to their relationships in general and not just in there love life.

The Length of Line

Excessively Long Line

If your subject's heart line stretches all the way across its hands, it's classified as excessively long, and it usually indicates a developed emotional nature. They are governed by their love and affection for others but they are always seeking to wrap themselves up with the affections of others and are very possessive, which could be a disadvantage because these kinds of people tend to be very jealous.

Long Line

If the heart line starts at the center of mount Jupiter, it can be considered a long line. The reading is pretty much the same with those who have an excessively long heart line; they are also governed by love. These kinds of people are affectionate and loving but they also expect a lot in return and can be very hurt when they are unappreciated.

Short Line

If the heart line starts on the mount of Saturn it is considered a short line. These kinds of people tend to love nature and also seek for a mate, but they are more concerned about their personal desires. According to many experts, those who possess a short length heart line are sensual people, however, they are not motivated by love and compassion; it is mostly coming from a sexual desire and a need for a partner or companion.

Very Short Line

If the heart line begins on the mount of Apollo it is considered a very short length heart line. It usually indicates that a person is emotionally cold and don't care about other people's well-being. They usually form selfish relationships or the kind of relationship that just serves their own purpose. If they give something they want something in return, they don't give things out of love or generosity; they only do it because they have their own agenda.

General Information about the Heart Line

A clear line from start to finish indicates that a person is emotionally consistent and will have a rewarding emotional life.

Broad and shallow lines mean that a person's love nature is shallow and insincere, and their emotional life will not be meaningful or rewarding.

A thin line in proportion to other lines on the hand shows an emotionally self – centered person or has a selfish personality.

An island in the heart line will show a period of instability, unsettledness and maybe undergoing emotional difficulty. Your subject may currently have divided feelings.

Chained heart line (series of islands) in the palm will show extended periods of unsettledness and emotional difficulty.

A break in the line will show a complete change in your subject's emotional disposition. This could be brought about by being badly let down or discouraged by someone they loved.

A dot or hollows in the line has a bad significance because it shows a sudden and intense period of emotional difficulty.

Little lines that rise into the heart line are positive and usually indicate affections or friendships will come into their lives or they will experience it.

Split lines that fall away from the heart line are negative, and usually indicate emotional depressions. If you happen to see a split line, it signifies that an emotional drain will last for as long as it continues to run underneath the heart line.

A jumbled heart line or confused character of the line indicates that a person's emotional nature may also be jumbled or they are undergoing a rollercoaster of emotions.

Red Line

If the heart line is reddish in color, it indicates an increase in the intensity of the person's emotional nature as well as the relative strength of the line.

Pink Line

This indicates a warm and compassionate person, especially towards their friends and loved ones.

White Line

Just like the palm color, white heart line indicates coldness. If the line is very long, the subject will tend to be self-contained and does not always show compassion.

Active and Passive Hand

- If the heart line is much clearer and longer in your subject's active hand, it's an indicator that he/she has become a more loving, compassionate and selfless person over the years.

- If the heart line is much clearer and longer in your subject's passive hand it usually indicates that he/she had gone through some life experience that made him/her become less affectionate and less inclined to be giving in their emotional life.

Timing of Events

The timing of events for the line of heart can be very difficult. In fact, many expert palmists are still arguing on where they could base the starting point to determine the date of certain readings. According to modern palmists, split lines are the starting point for the same of consistency, simplicity and coherence. However, many traditionalists disagree with the idea, and they say that the starting line should be on the mount of Jupiter. The nature of the line under Jupiter can vary dramatically from hand to hand, and as previously mentioned it is during childhood that a person's foundation was set in stone which is why   the mount of Jupiter is regarded as the most logical starting point for this line.

According to many palmists, it is quite possible to date events on lines that are fairly clear and consistent through measuring the line and then dividing its length by seventy (to get the amount of space occupied by one year) so that one can achieve satisfying results, particularly in regards to a subject's past events. The curve of this line often makes it difficult to measure, but you can apply a simple method.

You can set a small pair of dividers to a spacing of one centimeter and then measure the line of heart from start to finish. After determining its length you can then set the dividers to ten year intervals (normally 0.9 to 1.2 centimeters) and work your way through the line using your judgment and knowledge to gauge the exact year of any marks or changes to the character of the line. However, people's emotional nature are complex which is why a detailed analysis of past and future events is extremely difficult and only major prints can be taken into consideration.

So if you decide to experiment with this kind of method or any other method for that matter, you have to be very cautious and careful when trying to predict future events for your customers or subjects.

Chapter Five: The Line of Head

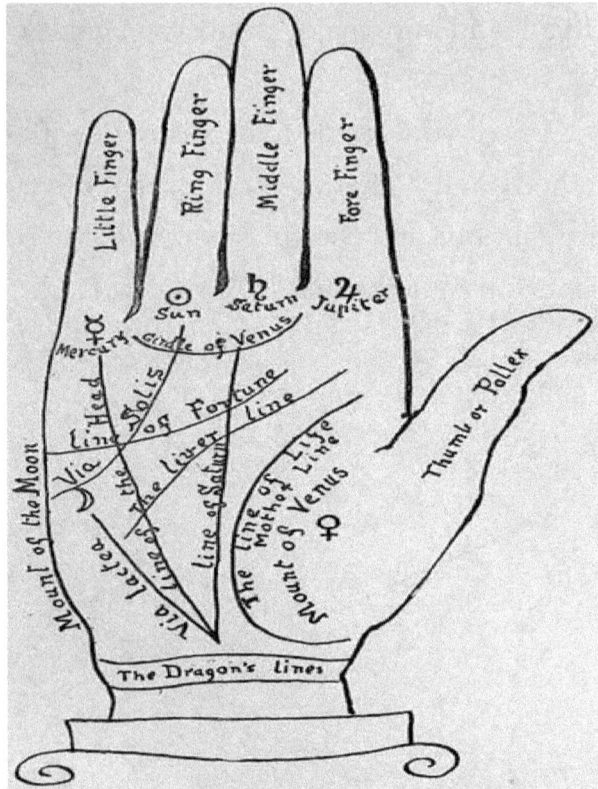

The Head Line indicates your subject's mental energies and rationalization powers. It also covers the scope of their mentality, how they think, and the kinds of decisions they make. Expert believes the Head Line shows a person's degree of intelligence, but nothing could be further from the truth.

Although long, clear and well-formed head lines are often seen on the hands of very intelligent people, they are also often seen on the hands of unintelligent ones! A person's degree of intelligence is indicated by the physical aspects of their hand, particularly the middle part of the thumb. The head line only points out a person's ability to put their intelligence to use by responding to what they think how they make plans or decide on something, and act on them. In this chapter we will cover the different factors to consider for you to accurately read a palm. We'll discuss the significance and indications of the head line's length as well as some general information.

The Length of Line

The longer the head line the greater the scope of your subject's mentality and the more they are influenced by what they think. The shorter the line the shorter the scope of their mentality and the less their life is influenced or regulated by what they think. Here's the indication of each length of the head line:

Excessively Long Line

It stretches all the way across the hand and shows someone who is ruled by their mentality. They rationalize everything in all the aspects of their life to what they think. However, this also means that the person limits themselves to what their mind can only deal with and anything that is beyond the scope of their mentality, is blocked out or ignored. These kinds of people are very analytic and calculating; they cannot cope, and if they cannot escape, they could suffer a mental break down.

Long Line

It is almost the same with excessively long lines but they are not quite so limited by their mentality. They are able to make good use of the mentality they have, but are also inclined to be too rational in their plans and approach to life.

Medium Line

Medium length head line indicates that your subject's rational thinking is adequately developed. They are able to make good use of the mentality they have, but they are not limited by a need to be rational and far sighted in everything they do or plan. These kinds of people have a good control over their mentality, but there is no question of too much mental control or of the life being limited by a need to rationalize everything.

Short Line

A short length head line indicates that a person does not have enough control over their life. Their mind lacks the capacity to make full use of the available intelligence and they are short-sighted in their decisions, they are also not long – term planners.

Very Short Line

This only means that your subject has a limited mentality. So if there's any indication of intelligence by other aspects of the hand, it usually has little to no use. These kinds of people are also poor in making long – term decisions, because they have a one – track mind. They may be an expert about one subject but they know nothing about anything else including their other life aspects.

General Information about the Head Line

A line that is clear, and well - defined throughout its length means that your subject has clarity of thought, continuity of purpose, good memory, and an ability to exercise self-control.

A broad and shallow line indicates mental inertia or a kind of person who allows themselves to drift through life without any clear path. They are the "go with the flow" type.

A thin line shows they are unable to withstand much mental stress or pressure from various life events.

An island shows a period of mental instability. The person is divided in their thoughts, and they could be very inconsistent in their decisions. When you see defects on the head line you must make also consider the strength of the Mount of Luna as defects on this island on the head line. Lines are much more serious when the Mount of Moon/Luna is strongly developed, this will tell you whether or not your subject recovers completely.

A chain in your subject's palm indicates a period of time when the mentality is divided, or unsettled.

An incidental line that starts on the mount of Jupiter and joins the head line some way down the hand shows the time when the person became very mentally ambitious.

Split Lines

Split lines that leave the head line and run the chained head line in an upward direction show the period when the person tries to develop a greater mental control over their life.

Split lines that falls from the heart line and merges with the head line means that a difficult emotional decision has been made in favor of the head and not the heart.

Split lines that droop from the head line show the pulling power of the imagination on your subject's mentality. The person dreams and hopes, but because the head line continues on its pre-determined path their goals or dreams remain unfulfilled most of the time.

Active and Passive Hand

- If the active hand's head line is has a much clearer print than the passive hand that usually means that your subject has learnt to make better use of their mentality, is more of a rational thinker and more consistent in their decisions.

- People who have a straighter head line in their active hand often experiences financial difficulties, a palmist should advise them to be more practical, and realistic so that they can control of their finances. On the other hand, those who have a sloping head line in their active hand don't have a problem with their finances; money comes easily for them because they were able to allow themselves to be more imaginative and idealistic.

Timing of Events

Dating events on the line of head is also extremely difficult for many experts. You can have some degree of success on lines that are clear and well-marked from beginning to end, however it still may not be that accurate.

Perhaps one of the main problems why many palmists, both traditional and modernist, cannot establish guidelines that can be relied upon is because people undergo changes to the way they think without consciously realizing that they are changing.

There can be a noticeable time difference between the time an individual begins to change the way they think, and the time they realize that changes have occurred. And because there are a lot of subtleties and factors involved, creating a clear and reliable system for dating events will have to wait until a fully equipped research team of palmists and experts find a way and be able to justify it. Like the method used in the line of heart, the length of the line equals seventy years and by dividing that length by seventy, a palmist or a practitioner may be able to establish how much distance is occupied by each year.

Chapter Six: The Line of Life

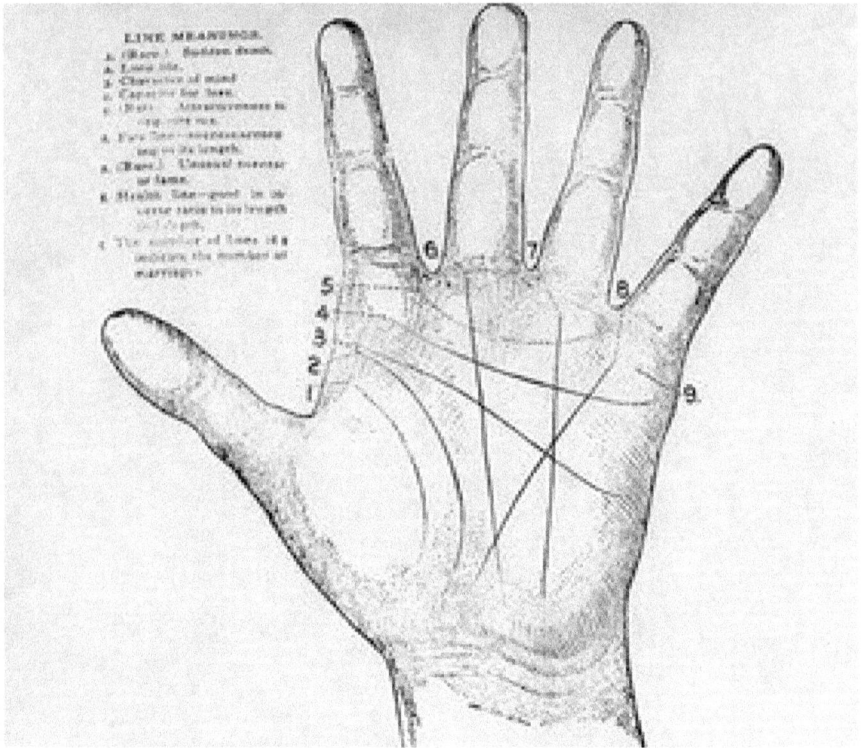

The life line relates to the physical aspects of a person's nature, but there are many subtleties involved which is why it's important to consider other factors before making a final reading or prediction. The life line also shows your subject's strength, health, and physical vitality. It can also indicate the effect of these matters on the kind of life they live, its quality, and whether or not they are likely to have children.

In this chapter we will cover the different factors to consider for you to accurately read a palm. We'll discuss the significance and indications of the life line, its relation to the active and passive hand as well as some general information.

General Characteristics

The life line starts from the side of the hand between the mounts of Jupiter and lower Mars, and then curves around the mount of Venus, and ends at the wrist. Generally speaking, the longer the line the longer the period in which the person can be expected to enjoy physical vitality up to their old age; the shorter the line the shorter the period in which they can rely on their physical vitality, or will soon depend on someone to care for them. You might encounter a palm that has no life line, although this is very rare, there are still some people who don't have it. If so, it usually indicates that your subject lacks vitality, physically weak, tends to get ill easily, and mostly survives only because of their nervous energy.

Even if the life line is an indicator of one's vitality and longevity, it doesn't always mean that one will live longer if they have a long length, and it also doesn't mean that those who have shorter life line will die at a much younger age or will lack in physical vitality.

General Information about Life Line

The depth and clarity of the line is important to notice. A deep and clear line indicates that your subject has a great deal of physical vitality and lives a rewarding life.

A broad and shallow line indicates a diminished vitality, and although the person does the thing they like or take pleasure in, they do not find their life rewarding.

Thin life line indicates someone who cannot endure a hardship and someone who gets easily tired when they try to exert themselves physically in something.

If the line undergoes a slight change of direction it will indicate a change in lifestyle. If it suddenly starts to adopt a greater outward curve then the lifestyle is more active. If it suddenly begins to curve in on the mount of Venus then it means that the lifestyle is less active and more restricted.

If you find a break in the life line, it signifies something serious and it also shows a break in the physical energy flow. Although often the result of illness or accident, this is not always the case as a break sometimes corresponds with a complete change in the lifestyle of a person.

A dot on the line usually relates to your subject's health. The dots indicates an interruption in your subject's energy flow, and the deeper or more clearly it is marked, the more serious the indication.

An island shows a division of the energies and a period of difficulty in life. The person is unsettled and although an island often follows a defect such as a dot, it sometimes indicates the person simply feels drained and is unable to make the effort to get their life organized.

A chained line shows extended periods of difficulty which affects either the person's health or personal well-being.

A laddered line in the life line indicates a weak physical constitution. Your subject lacks vitality and should be advised to avoid stressful situations, their energy levels are usually unstable and they often get exhausted. Many people with weak, thin, or laddered life lines also have difficulty finding their ideal mates.

Energy Lines

Energy lines sometimes leave the life line and rise up towards one of the energy line rising to the mount of Jupiter. These lines are always good to see because they indicate that a person makes considerable efforts to improve themselves or achieve a particular goal.

If the palm has an energy line with soft consistency, it usually indicates that he/she strives to overcome their laziness and also makes an effort to achieve their goals.

If one of the energy lines rises to Jupiter it shows the person makes an effort to rise and improve both themselves and their status in life.

If the energy line rises to Saturn it usually shows that they make a considerable effort to increase their financial security or status and material well-being.

Relation of Palm Colors in Life Line

As what was mentioned in the previous chapters, color is important to note because it can increase or decrease the severity of the condition.

A pinkish color of the life line reduces the severity of any defects in the line (such as dots, breaks, ladder etc). A reddish life line is also a good sign because it increases the intensity of the physical vitality. If you see a whitish mark, it indicates physical lethargy, even when the line is deep or well – marked.

Active and Passive Hand

- If the life line in the active hand is not as well marked as the passive one, then the person has not been taking care of their health. The person's system is being undermined, and as a palmist you should advise your customer/subject to pay more attention to their physical well-being.
- If the life line is marked in the active hand, it indicates that their physical side is stronger and is more resistant to diseases.

Timing of Events

The dating of events on the line of life is similar to timing of events on the line of head and heart. The only difference is that instead of measuring the actual length of the line, you should measure the normal distance it is expected to travel.

You can try using small dividers set to one centimeter; the line should be measured from its starting point around the mount of Venus, and down to the wrist. If it ends early you just simply follow its course. The measurement from the beginning to your subject's wrist covers about seventy years of life and by setting the dividers to ten year intervals you can gauge the timeframe through the line one decade at a time.

Chapter Seven: The Line of Fate

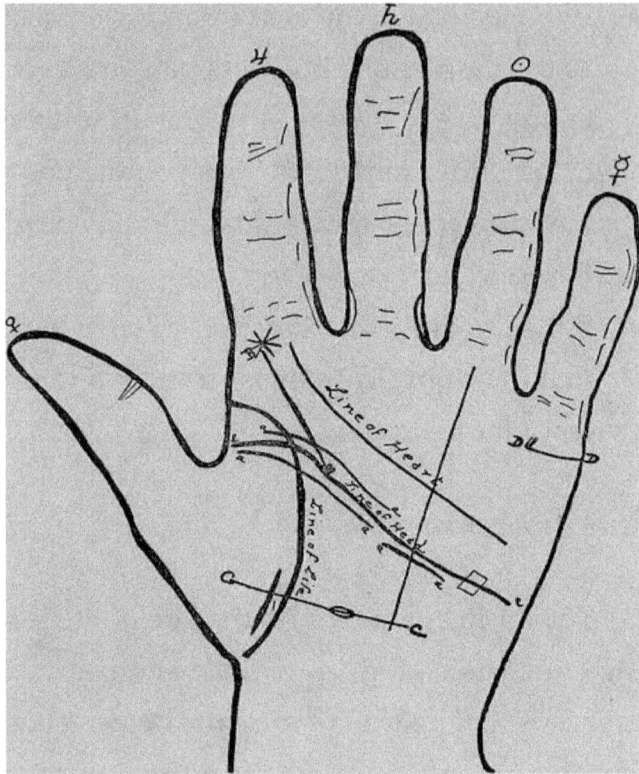

The line of fate, also known as the Saturn Line indicates the directional attitude of your subject and how that attitude is affected by various circumstances. The presence of a Fate Line shows that a person has a direction in life and he/she is working towards his/her goals and dreams, but if it is badly marked or defective (has breaking points, splits, dots etc.) in any way, it indicates that they are experiencing difficulty and failing to make the kind progress they would like to make.

This is a very valuable line because it relates to one's life purpose and what they worked so far to achieve their goals. If the line of fate is clear and well-marked it indicates they find satisfaction in what they are doing and feel that they are making progress in life. If you ever encounter a palm that doesn't have a line of fate, it shows that your subject have no direction in life and they only pretty much live to exist and not the other way around.

In this chapter we will cover the different factors to consider for you to accurately read a palm. We'll discuss the significance and indications of the fate line, its relation to the active and passive hand as well as some general information.

General Information about the Fate Line

If the fate line is clear and well-marked it indicates their work life or career is going well and they feel they are making progress.

If the line is broad and shallow it indicates that your subject may be struggling in life, cannot find their "break" or right opportunities, and dissatisfied with the trend of events.

Any defects in the line show difficulties in the career or direction in life.

An island in the fate line indicates a time of great difficulty and that the person is divided and unsettled during that particular period, on the other hand, a chain shows an extended period of great difficulty.

Sections of the line that are very deep show periods of great struggles and stresses in the career or direction of life.

A dot in the line usually indicates a period of sudden, unexpected difficulty. The condition of the line after the dot will show how it affected the direction or career of the individual.

An offshoot or branch line that rises from the line of fate and heading towards the Mount of Apollo shows the person's idea of their success is considerably enhanced, but the kind of success depends very much on their personal sense of values. If the line rises towards Jupiter then it shows an increase in status or authority and the person has a greater ability to influence others and control events. These branch lines are also indicates a short period of increased success, but if they are long and rise to the mount then the period of increased success is long lasting!

A small line joining the line of fate indicates the individual's directional attitude was influenced by another person.

An influence line that fails to join the fate line and just rises up alongside indicates that the influence gives a huge assistance to a person's career or direction in life.

It is common to see a weak fate Line which grows considerably clearer and stronger after being joined by an influence line. This is often a sign of marriage showing that the union gave the person some real purpose and sense of direction in life.

If the fate line grows thinner or weaker and if it also crosses the head line, it indicates that after a certain age the person began to lose interest in maintaining their life's direction or pursuing a certain goal.

A deep, well-marked fate Line that goes straight to the Mount of Saturn and is not joined by any influence lines indicates that an individual is someone who is quite lonely in life, and only their career or body of work is important to them. They concentrate so much on what they are doing and where they want to go that they ignore other equally important aspects of life such as family, relationships, worldly purpose etc. Anything that interferes with their direction or slows their progress will be subconsciously avoided including marriage and friendships. However, if your subject does get married, his/her marriage will only be secondary to their careers. If there will be conflicts their careers and own personal direction will win.

A grill on Saturn is a bad sign, even if the fate line is clear and well-marked. In such a case the person has direction and purpose in life, but they will not do that well as they expected, and could also be very slow in their progress.

If there's a hollow in the center of the hand it often signifies a bad sign concerning material things. The hollow is the result of a deficient plain of Mars showing the person doesn't like to confront such circumstances. But if they don't stand up for themselves when they should, a much difficult situations may arise, which could make them harder to be successful in life.

Crossbar Lines

A crossbar is a negative sign and shows interference to the natural direction of life.

When it is followed by a weakening or thinning of the line it indicates the interference causes the person to lose their momentum and interest in maintaining their direction. It is not unusual to see a crossbar followed by a weakening of the line which in turn is followed by a break. In such a case it means that the interference has caused a loss of interest and momentum in one's life, which in turn is followed by a temporary loss of direction.

If the new line is placed differently the change may indicate a result in a change of job or career.

Breaking Lines

A break is a serious matter. If the line of your subject just stops and then starts again a short time it indicates that an individual loses their direction for a period of time

If a new line is placed differently on the hand or goes in a different direction then there is a complete change in the life direction of the individual.

If the breaking lines overlap with other lines it indicates a gradual change in a person's life direction.

If there is no overlapping of the lines then the change is sudden and may even be unexpected.

Whenever you're dealing with breaks in the line of fate, it's very important to remember that a change of attitude is generally the result of something that happens in life. A person who finds their direction meaningful is unlikely to feel any need to change their attitude, compared to someone who is experiencing problems or difficulties because he/she is much more likely to reconsider their where their life is going which could prompt them to make a change.

Active and Passive Hand

- If the line in the active hand is clearer and better marked than the one in the passive, it indicates the person carefully plans their career and direction in life and is may likely achieved a greater degree of success.

- If the line in the active hand is not as clear or well-marked as to the passive hand, then the situation is simply reversed.

Timing of Events

Timing the line of fate is much easier because there is no curve to it compared to other major lines in the palm. The distance from the apex of Mount of Saturn to the base of the palm is seventy years.

As usual once you have measured that distance you can use a small pair of dividers to gauge the time period one decade at a time. The length of the line should be divided by seventy and multiplied by ten is equivalent to the distance of ten years.

You can also try determining the distance occupied by each year by dividing the length by seventy to determining the age of your subject's event (Length of the line of heart divided by seventy = year). You can then measure the distance from the apex of the Mount of Saturn to the point you are interested in, divide that measurement by the year figure, and then subtract your result from seventy. (Apex of Saturn to point of interest = distance. Distance divided by year = years from seventy. Seventy minus years from seventy = age of event.)

However, like on other lines, determining the time period or date of every event cannot be accurately measured. Even expert palmists can only give the approximate year of any mark or change to the fate line.

Chapter Eight: The Line of Success

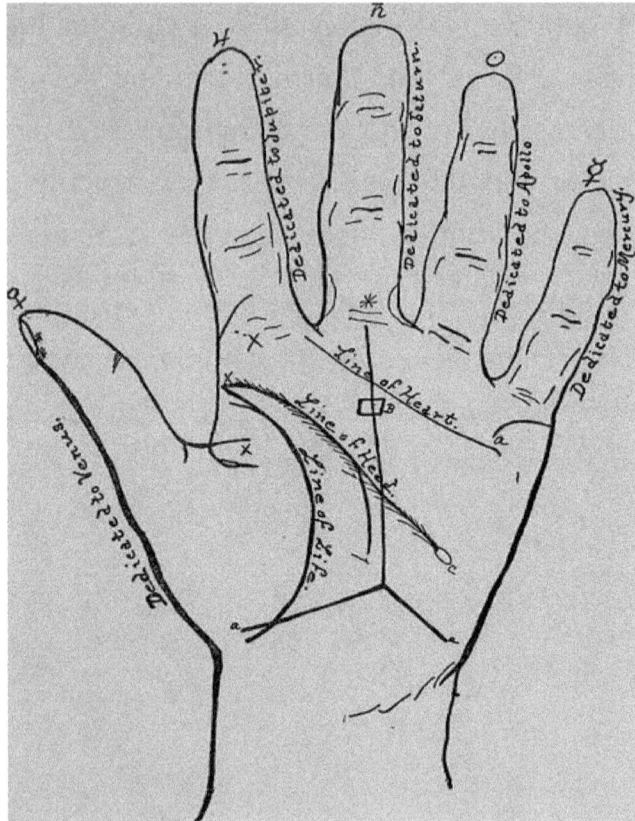

When it comes to the line of success, or otherwise called as the Line of Apollo, the important thing to remember is that it indicates success from the point of view of an individual, and not from of a worldly perspective or how society defines success. So this in fact can be considered as the line of personal success. If you see this mark on the hand of your subject it indicates that he/she is able to live the life they want to live, and are also in a position to do things that expresses their own sense of individuality.

You may also get to encounter subjects that doesn't have a success line but still managed to do very well, and someone who may have even become extremely successful to the point that they're getting acclaimed internationally for their achievements. However, in such cases, no matter how successful these people are and no matter how much satisfaction they may get from their success, the absence of the line of Apollo therefore indicates that they do not achieve the kind of success they would like to achieve and are unable to live the kind of life they would like to live, it's like they didn't got what they want on their own terms. On the other hand, a person who makes a modest living by doing what they want to do is likely to feel personally successful and this personal success will be shown by the line of Apollo printed on their palms.

General Information about the Line of Success

If your subject's line of success is deeper, clearer, and well-marked, it indicates a greater degree of personal success. However, it is the comparative strength of this line that has to be carefully considered.

In a case where the line is clear, well-marked, and quite prominent, your subject can expect to have a high degree of personal success. In fact, he/she can likely achieve fame and ultimate recognition. On the other hand, if the lines of Apollo are weak and thin or kind of fading, it indicates a limited degree of personal success.

A palmist can determine or at least gauge the age at which feelings of personal success begin by looking at the starting point of the Apollo line. Often this line doesn't start until quite high in the hand showing that it takes many years for the person to develop their life to a point where they can begin to feel personally successful.

If a palmist encounters a line that starts low on the hand, then an individual have already enjoyed some form of personal success at a young age by some form of luck or probably with other people's help. Most of the time though, palmists see a thin line starting very high on the hand which usually indicates that a person is only able to do the things they want to do and live the life they want to live after they have retired.

If you see single vertical line that is clear and well - marked on the mount of Apollo it usually indicates that no matter how artistic or creative the person is, because the line appears only on the mount of Apollo, they will not achieve personal success until late in life.

If the line of success rises on Upper Mars, it indicates that success eventually comes from dogged persistence. Your subject will likely have to try many times and may go through many failures before they get what they want in life

If you see an island, dot or crossbar on the line of Apollo, it usually indicates that an individual will undergo some form of difficulty before achieving personal success.

An island is an extended period of difficulty, a dot is something sudden and unexpected, and a crossbar shows some form of interference. Just like the defects on any line, the quality of the line of success after a defect must be considered to determine whether or not the difficulty has any long lasting effects on the person or your subject.

If you see a well-marked star on the line of Apollo, it is usually considered as indicator of great fame and success, but very few people achieve the kind of success and personal acclaim they wish for.

If there is no fate line in your subject's hand, the line of Apollo can compensate for that, but it usually indicates that a person spends their time living in the present or at the moment, and doing what they enjoy doing than considering the future. However, if the line of Apollo is stronger, then it indicates that their desire to do the things they want to do and live the life they want to live is stronger than their desire to continue developing their life along desired lines of the fate line.

If the line of fate is the stronger than the two it means that although the person's desire to develop their life along the desired lines is accompanied by feelings of personal success, they still do not feel quite as personally successful as they would like to.

If the line of Apollo goes towards Saturn it usually indicates that your subject tries to use their personal success to promote something they are serious about and something that is important to them.

Timing of Events

The method used in timing events in the line of success or the line of Apollo is just the same with measuring the line of fate. The distance from the apex of the Mount of Apollo to the base of the palm is seventy years and each mark can be calculated using the same method previously given in the chapter of the line of fate (see previous chapter).

Chapter Nine: The Line of Marriage and Children

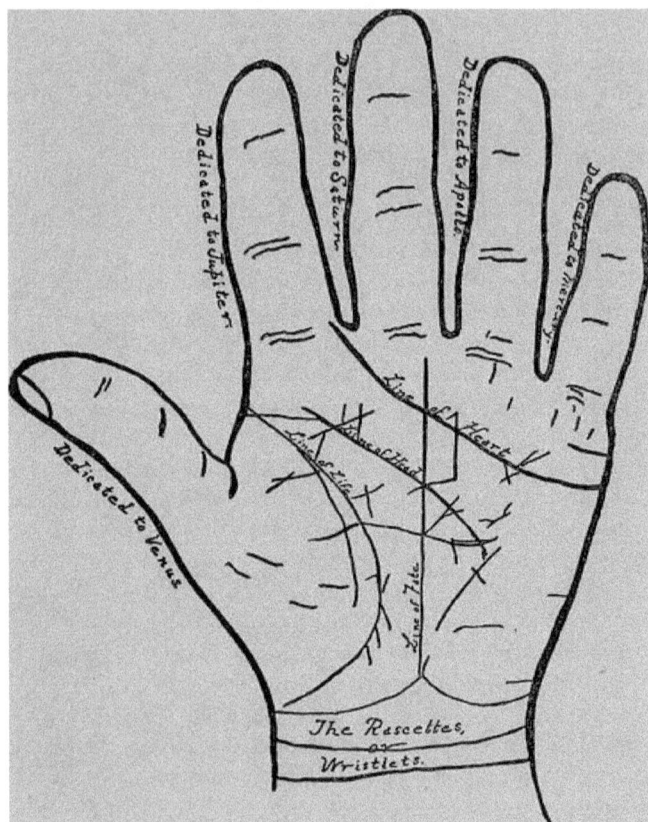

Traditional and modern palmists have found that the traditional meanings of these lines are very unreliable, and it's also quite impossible to determine exactly and accurately when an individual will get married or when they're going to have children or how many will it be. According to them, different people get married and have kids for different reasons.

This is why most palmists tries to determine first why their subject will get married in the first place – is it because they love their current partner, or is it for other personal reasons? Or why they wanted to have kids. This can enable them to know which part of the hand to read.

Even if there are many instances when a marriage line accurately translates to a real – life marriage, there are still a lot of instances where it doesn't. If it does though, you can probably call that luck or just a co-incidence for the palmist's part because most of the time realities do not match the number of marriage lines on their subject's hand.

Marriage Lines

Marriage lines appear as very short lines on the side of the hand under the pinkie finger and above the line of heart. They can also be long lines that rise from the side towards the mount of Mercury; sometimes it even goes further into the palm itself. Such lines indicate that a subject communicates with another person in a special way.

If the marriage line is well – marked, it means that there is greater degree of communication, and if the lines are deep and clear, it usually indicates a very intimate relationship.

If the deep line is close to the heart line, it indicates that a person will get married at an early age.

Happy marriage lines should be clear and straight without splits or islands in it. It is also often found lying on the mount of Mercury.

If the line curves downwards, your subject will outlive his/her partner or spouse.

If the line turns upward in a reverse direction, an individual may not get married.

If the line is clear but has drooping little lines, it could mean troubles in marriage because of an illness.

If the line is well – marked but has break in two, it foreshadows a break – up or fatality in a happy married life.

If the marriage line joins the line of the sun or line of success, it usually indicates that the subject will marry someone who is rich or has some form of distinction. However, if the same kind of line bends and cuts the line of success, it means that the subject will lose position in the marriage he/she will have.

If the line of Mercury falls into the line of marriage, it indicates that there'll be great obstacles in the marriage that needs to be overcome.

If lines crosses the mount of Mars and rises up towards the marriage line, it usually indicates that there'll be interferences in the marriage.

Islands

If there's an island at the start, it usually indicates that the marriage will be delayed for a very long time and they could also be separated during the duration of their married life. An example is if the spouse is working abroad or based far away.

If the island is lying on the middle of the line of marriage, it means that a separation will likely happen in the middle of their married life.

If the island is lying on the end of the line of marriage, it indicates that the marriage will have an unfortunate ending, and also separation.

If the line of marriage consists of little islands or chains, the subject should be warned not to get married at any time soon because the marriage will be full of unhappiness.

Fork Lines

If the line of marriage divides into a fork, then the couple will likely live apart but if the fork is turn downwards to the line of heart, a legal separation may occur.

If the fork line is accentuated, and if one end of the fork goes towards the mount of Mars, the marriage may end up in divorce.

However, what a lot palmist can't say or can't determine is if that particular relationship is marital, sexual or maybe just platonic.

When it comes to these kinds of matter, it must be handled with caution because many people are sensitive about their love or relationship nature, a subject may tell you about their marriage but they may not discuss other details like their previous affairs or relationships or people they loved and cared for but chose not to get involved with. The complexities involved pertaining to intimate relationships can be quite difficult and unreliable. Be honest with your subject if you really can't read or interpret their marriage line.

You can also refer to the line of fate from previous chapters because it is related to affection and love.

Children Lines

These lines are extremely unreliable, so much so that most competent palmists now ignore them completely. Although there are occasions when, on the hand of an older person, the numbers of children lines accurately reflect the number of children they have had, these instances are rare. The accumulation of knowledge is an ongoing process and in time, new information is likely to allow a palmist to deal with the question of children more accurately, but for the present, it is wiser for the student to refrain from trying to use these lines to predict the number of children a person will have.

The lines relating to children are found above the line of marriage. It is usually clear and fine upright lines. These lines are extremely and deeply marked, and are often found in women than men.

If the lines are broad and deep it usually indicates son/sons, if the lines are fine and narrow, the person/couple will give birth to daughters.

If the line is straight, it usually indicate strong and healthy kids, but if the lines are crooked or almost fading, it means that the children will be very delicate when it comes to their health.

If the little lines have small islands, the child will get ill at an early age, but if the line becomes well – marked passed this islands, then the child will get better and stronger or most likely recover. If the line is broken or has an ending, it may indicate that the child will not grow up, which also means that he/she will die at some point.

If one of the lines will stand out, or are better marked than other little lines, that means that this child will be of more importance to the parents, or he/she will be more successful than his/her siblings.

Chapter Ten: Minor Marks and Conclusion

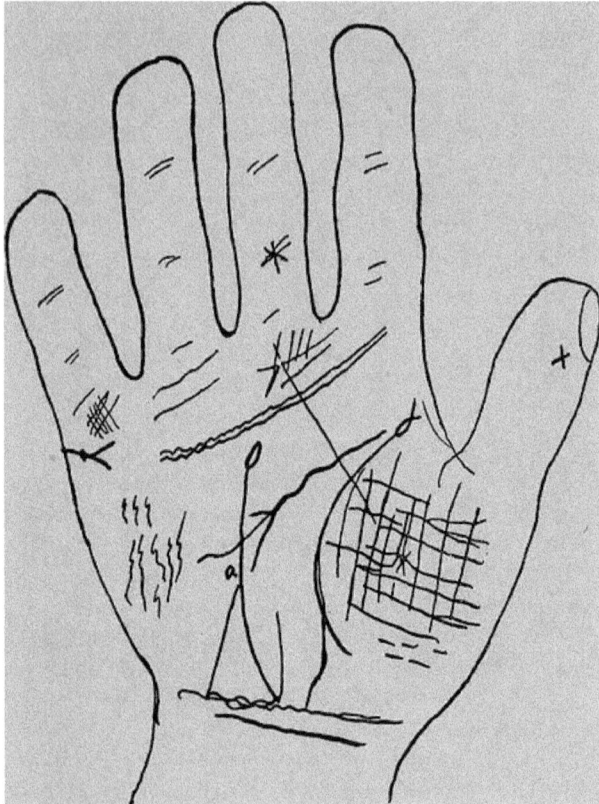

Now that you have learned the indications of the palm's major lines, in this chapter you will be given information about the interpretations of various marks usually found lying on the lines and on the different mounts. You will also be given some reminders on what to do before you and your subject proceed in analyzing the palm to achieve a more accurate reading, and be well on your way in becoming a proficient palm reader.

The Circle

Finding a circle in one's palm is extremely rare, in case you encounter a subject with a circle mark on its hands, it indicates negative or unfortunate circumstances. Many palmists consider it an evil mark, however if it is found on the mount of the Sun it can be considered favorable.

If the circle mark touches any lines or any other mounts it usually indicates something unfavorable or a misfortune to any line it crosses or touches. In palmistry, circles usually indicate an ongoing event that a person cannot easily escape or breakthrough. If the circle is located on the mount of the Moon or mount of Luna, an individual may die due to drowning.

The Spot

Spot marks usually indicate a chronic disease or illness. If it touches a line, it means a temporary illness can occur.

If the spot is found on the line of head, it indicates shock or head injuries. If the spot touches the line of life it signifies a sudden illness, if it's located particularly on the line of health it indicates a fever. Usually it is of no major significance if the spot is found on other lines of the palm.

The Grille

According to many palmists, grille marks is the point where energy escapes, so if you found grille marks all over the hand or your subject's entire palm it usually indicates that the person's energy and power is always getting drained and may also dissipates.

If the grille mark touches any mount, it saps the energy qualities of the mount. It also indicates that the person will undergo through many obstacles in life that is related to the particular mount it touches or represents. An example is if the grille is found on the mount of Apollo, there'll be lack of success on the quality of the mount it symbolizes.

The Star

The star is generally a good symbol because it denotes brilliance and great things in one's life.

If a line ends in a star, it usually indicates that the person can achieve the greatest accomplishment in his/her life. However, as what the saying goes, "success always comes with a price." The star symbol may also mean that it carries with it an unpleasant price.

If it is found on the mount of Jupiter, it means added glory, power and possession.

If it is found on the mount of Sun, it promises riches and also glory although it is mostly associated to public life.

If it is found on the mount of Mercury, it means having success in corporate or business endeavors, scientific endeavors, depending on the palm's other indications.

If it is found on the mount of Mars that is under the mount of Jupiter, it indicates that the person will have great distinction in his/her marital life, or the person will undergo some battle that will boost the stature of his/her career.

If it is found on the mount of Mars that is under the mount of Mercury, it usually gives an honor that is won by conquering one's life, or having to overcome personal issues.

If it is found on the mount of Moon/Luna, it's a sign of great celebrity arising depending on the qualities of the mount.

If the star is found on the mount of Saturn, it usually indicates unfavorable circumstances to a person's life. It does give distinction but it will be one that is dreaded. The person or your subject will be casts as part of some terrible tragedy of life. His/her life will most likely end up in tragedy or a really unfortunate disaster that will cause his/her name to be remembered or have a distinction but for unfortunate reasons. An example is a king crowned by doom.

The Cross

A cross generally indicates a form of trouble like danger, or disappointment. If it is found on lines, some palmists say that the bearer will have burdens similar to the Holy Cross of Jesus. Sometimes it can also mean a dramatic change in one's life because of a crisis, traumatic event, or hardship.

The only favorable indication of a cross is, if it is found on the mount of Jupiter. This means that the person will be extremely fortunate in terms of affection that will come into his/her life. If it is found on the other mounts, it denotes unfavorable circumstances.

The person will end up in a violent death, if the sign is on the mount of Saturn.

There'll be disappointment in money or fortunes if found on the mount of the Sun.

Dishonesty will occur if found on the mount of Mercury.

There'll be great opposition if found on the mount of Mars that is under the mount of Mercury.

If it is found of the mount of Mars under the mount of Jupiter, it usually indicates a violent death because of quarrels.

If a cross is on the mount of Luna, it means that a person will deceive himself, and will cause fatal influence to one's imagination. If the cross is found on the lower part of the mount, it means death due to drowning.

If the cross in on the mount of Venus, it means that there'll be some fatal influence related to affections.

If the cross is above the head line, it indicates a head injury or accident.

If the cross is above the heart line, it indicates a loved one's sudden death.

The Square

The square, also known as the mark of Preservation, is always a good symbol because it provides protection from experiencing unfortunate indications brought about my chain, split or dotted lines in the palm. Although difficulties will still likely occur, the beholder will be able to avert the crisis and the damage will be reduced or even prevented.

If it is found of the life line, it indicates preservation from death, and if found on the fate line, there'll be preservation from loss depending also on the quality of the lines and its indications.

The Triangle

Another positive mark is the triangle because it is usually signifies strength (if it stands as an independent mark and does not have intersecting lines). It is formed by the head, life and heart line. It usually indicates mental and health flourishes as well as success depending on the line or mount it touches.

If it is found on the mount of Apollo, it signifies an artistic success. The larger the triangle, the better is the success depending on the lines or mounts it touches.

Triangles also signify balance, and will not carry any backlash unlike the star symbol.

The Quadrangle

It is a space that lies in the middle of the head line and the heart which forms a quadrangle. A well – marked quadrangle should be shaped – evenly and should not have a narrow end on the four corners. It also represents an individual's mental attitude towards other people.

Quadrangles denote balance in mentality, and judgment. If it is extremely narrow it means that there's narrowness in terms of their religious views. On the other hand, if it is excessively wide, it means lack of judgment, and a loose view for one's good.

Some Rules before Reading a Palm

Now that you have learn the basics of palmistry, and all its indications, the last thing you should learn for you to achieve best results is to make sure that your subject's palm is ready and have been "prepared" beforehand so you can clearly interpret it. Below are some rules that can help you prepare yourself as well as your subject's palm.

- As much as possible, don't touch the hand of your subject before you do any palm reading. Don't shake hands with them or pre-examine because the electric current of both your bodies can affect the genuine features of the hands and palm.

- You can see a palm anytime of the day, but many highly recommend that the best time to analyze one is in the morning preferably before eating breakfast or before they do anything major. The reason for this is that the digestion of food affects the blood circulation, and because of this the minor lines may become invisible after food intake or strenuous activities.

- It is also best if your subject and also you, the palm reader, had taken a bath before doing palmistry. This is to avoid hindrances in interpreting because a dirty or lazy body makes the atmosphere quite irrelevant.

- A palm reader should not read a palm that has either a very hot or cold temperature due to weather changes. The hand will obviously change its color depending on the outside condition which can affect the palm reading.

- Subjects should also not come in for a reading if he/she has taken alcoholic drinks or any intoxicants such as drugs etc. or if a person is not feeling well or is not in a healthy condition. This is why as a palmist you should talk to your subject first, get to know them a bit or ask what they did beforehand or why they decide to come to you. You can also go through a checklist of the things you should ask your subjects so as not to forget anything.

- A palmist should also not perform any reading if he/she is angry or not in a good state.

- Lastly, as a palmist, you should always examine a hand with the utmost concern. Even if the individual is a relative, a loved one or even an enemy. Don't let emotions rule out the basic readings of palmistry, otherwise your predictions will be most likely unrealistic. Tell it as you see it, don't cover the truth, and like most things in life, don't let your emotions cloud your judgment or in this case, your interpretations.

Conclusion

Palmistry is probably created or discovered as a way of making people believe in something that will raise their hopes up, and make them dream for a better future. Or perhaps it warns people, and gives them a heads up of what's to come through some of its negative implications. Whatever the reading may be, always remember that the future is not yet written, it will change for better or worse, and while the practice is still entirely unproven, I believe palmistry exists to remind people and tell them one clear message: your future is indeed in the palm of your hands!

Glossary of Palmistry Terms

Apex: The middle of the lines within the hand print

Apollo Finger: the hand's third finger.

Arch Pattern: resembles a humpback bridge in the line pattern.

Bar: a short ark or a horizontal line that denotes a hindrance

Bracelets: See Rascettes

Chain: consists of small islands that resemble a chain effect.

Chirognomy: The study of the basic shape of the hand.

Chiromancy: The study of the lines of the hand, other term for palmistry.

Composite Pattern: A variation of an arch, loop, or whorl that is a skin pattern.

Conic Hand: denotes a round – shaped hand

Creative Curve: A clear curve on the hand's outer side

Croix Mystique: A well – marked cross in the middle of the heart and head lines.

Cross: A mark that appears on the hand usually denoting troubles

Dermatoglyphics: The study of the skin pattern in the fingers and palm.

Digital Mounts: A prominence found in the palm and under the four fingers

Empty Hand: A palm with a few visible lines.

Family Ring: Usually a line that connects the thumb's second and third phalange

Fate Line: Begins at the wrist up to the middle finger's base

Full Hand: A palm with a vast complexity of crisscrossing lines.

Girdle of Venus: A semicircular broken lines that runs from the mount of Jupiter to the mounts of Mercury or Apollo.

Grille: These are small horizontal lines forming a grille pattern on the palm.

Head Line: A line that starts on the hand's radial side and sweeps across the entire palm

Health Line: Also known as Mercury line.

Heart Line: The line that curves to the percussion, and starts under the first finger.

Hepatica: Mercury line or Health line's ancient term.

Index Finger: also called the Jupiter finger.

Influence Marks: patterns and minor lines that can be seen on the entire palm.

Island: A round shape line that resembles an island and usually denotes weakness.

Jupiter Finger: also known as the index finger.

Life Line: It begins anywhere but usually curves around the mount of Venus going towards the wrist.

Life-Saving Cross: A cross that is ½ - 2 inches long that also touches the fate and life lines.

Loop Pattern: One of the skin patterns

Mars Line: A line that runs parallel to the life of line

Medical Stigmata: Consists of 4 – 5 vertical lines going towards the inner side of Mercury's mount

Medius Finger: The Saturn or second finger.

Mercury Line: The line that usually runs from inside the life line directly to the mount of Mercury.

Milieu Line: Another term for fate line.

Moons: A white half-moon shapes found on the base of the fingernails.

Mounts: A palm's fleshy prominence

Percussion: A hand's outer edge

Phalange: The finger joints section

Radial: The thumb or active side of the hand.

Rascettes: Lines that run across the whole wrist just below the palm, also known as bracelets.

Ridges: A mark that denotes stress, can either be vertical or horizontal

Saturn Finger: The second or the middle finger.

Simian Line: A combination of head and heart line fused into one.

Square: A formation of lines that may appear on the palm or fingers.

Star: A star-like formation of lines that may appear on the palm or fingers usually denoting success.

Sydney Line: A line of head that completely crosses the palm.

Tented Arch: A pattern resembling a tall loop

Triangle: A formation of lines that may appear on hands or fingers.

Ulna: also referred to as the percussion or instinctive side.

Via Lasciva: A small horizontal or semicircular line connecting the base of mount Venus and Moon.

Whorl: It's a series of concentric circles

Zone of Mars: Located in the middle of digital mounts and atop of mount Venus and Moon.

Photo Credits

Page 1 Photo by user Malcolm Lidbury (aka Pinkpasty) via Wikimedia Commons, <https://commons.wikimedia.org/wiki/File:Palmistry_Chiromancy_Palm_Reading.jpg>

Page 2 Photo by user Aadi Singh via Flickr.com, <https://www.flickr.com/photos/aadieffigy/6195027721/>

Page 12 Photo by user Mimi Anderson via Flickr.com, <https://www.flickr.com/photos/tragically_dork/2650186640/in/photostream/>

Page 21 Photo by user Double – M via Flickr.com, <https://www.flickr.com/photos/double-m2/3728989982/>

Page 47 Photo by user Double – M via Flickr.com, <https://www.flickr.com/photos/double-m2/3894652764/>

Page 56 Photo by user Sara Sirolli via Wikimedia Commons, <https://commons.wikimedia.org/wiki/File:Mounts-melbourne-hand-analysis.JPG>

Page 60 Photo by user Double – M via Flickr.com, <https://www.flickr.com/photos/double-m2/3728188793/in/photostream/>

Page 69 Photo by user Mrs J. B. Dale via Wikimedia Commons, <https://commons.wikimedia.org/wiki/File:Indian_Palmistry _Plate_3.jpg>

Page 77 Photo by user Wicker Paradise via Flickr.com, <https://www.flickr.com/photos/wicker-furniture/10103872566/>

Page 84 Photo by user Carl Louis Perin from the book Perin's Science of Palmistry: A Complete and Authentic Treatise. Published by Star Publishing Co. Digitizing Sponsor: Brigham Young University via Wikimedia Commons, <https://commons.wikimedia.org/wiki/File:Perin%27s_scienc e_of_palmistry;_a_complete_and_authentic_treatise_(1902)_(14759798446).jpg>

Page 93 Photo by user Carl Louis Perin from the book Perin's Science of Palmistry: A Complete and Authentic Treatise. Published by Star Publishing Co. Digitizing Sponsor: Brigham Young University via Wikimedia Commons, <https://commons.wikimedia.org/wiki/File:Perin%27s_scienc e_of_palmistry;_a_complete_and_authentic_treatise_(1902)_(14782443092).jpg>

Page 99 Photo by user Carl Louis Perin from the book Perin's Science of Palmistry: A Complete and Authentic Treatise. Published by Star Publishing Co. Digitizing Sponsor: Brigham Young University via Wikimedia Commons, <https://commons.wikimedia.org/wiki/File:Perin%27s_scienc e_of_palmistry;_a_complete_and_authentic_treatise_(1902)_(14759822466).jpg>

Page 106 Photo by user Carl Louis Perin from the book Perin's Science of Palmistry: A Complete and Authentic Treatise. Published by Star Publishing Co. Digitizing Sponsor: Brigham Young University via Wikimedia Commons, <https://commons.wikimedia.org/wiki/File:Perin%27s_scienc e_of_palmistry;_a_complete_and_authentic_treatise_(1902)_(14782823155).jpg>

References

"A Beginner's Guide to Reading Palms"
Refinery29.com
<http://www.refinery29.com/palm-reading-guide-hand-
    lines-meaning>

"Everyone's Guide to Palmistry" PsychInternational.com
<http://www.psychicinternational.com/download/epalm.pdf
    >

"Exploring Lines on Your Palm" Thought.com
<https://www.thoughtco.com/palm-reading-lines-4051982>

"Hand Reading: An Introduction to Hand Analysis"
by Nasi Vadi via Hamsderser.dk
<http://hamderser.dk/handreadingbook.pdf>

"History of Palmistry - Continuation" Palmistry.com.au
<http://www.palmistry.com.au/history_of_palmistry.html>

"Moore's Manual of Up-to-date Palmistry" by Michael P.
    Moore via MysticKnowlede.org
<http://www.mysticknowledge.org/Moore_s_Manual_of_up
    -to-date_Palmistry.pdf>

"Palmistry" Links2theOccult.co.ok
<http://www.links2theoccult.co.uk/palmistry.pdf>

"Palmistry" Wikipedia.org
<https://en.wikipedia.org/wiki/Palmistry>

"Palmistry for All" by Cheiro via Deceptionary.com
 <https://www.deceptionary.com/ftp/Cheiro.pdf>

"Pamistry Lines through History" by Gary Markwick via
PalmistryinHand.com
<http://palmistryinhand.com/history-palmistry>

"Palmistry Terms and Definitions" Astrology Research
Foundation
<http://astrologyresearchfoundation.weebly.com/10-
palmistry-terms-and-definitions.html>

"Speed Palmistry" by Pt. V.R. Sharma via
    Akharpaybaydin.wordpress.com
<https://akharpaybaydin.files.wordpress.com/2011/06/speed-
    palmistry1.pdf>

"The Handbook of Palmistry" by Rosa Baughan via
IAPSOP
<http://www.iapsop.com/ssoc/1883__baughan___handbook_
of_palmistry.pdf>

**"Understanding Palmistry and What Your Hands Say
About You"** Exemplore.com
<https://exemplore.com/fortune-divination/Palmistry-What-
do-your-hands-say-about-you>

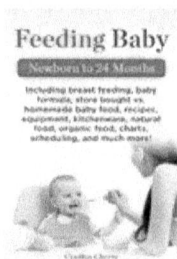

Feeding Baby
Cynthia Cherry
978-1941070000

Axolotl
Lolly Brown
978-0989658430

Dysautonomia, POTS
Syndrome
Frederick Earlstein
978-0989658485

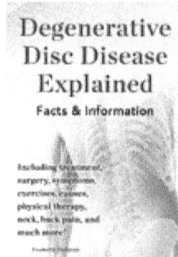

Degenerative Disc
Disease Explained
Frederick Earlstein
978-0989658485

Sinusitis, Hay Fever,
Allergic Rhinitis Explained
Frederick Earlstein
978-1941070024

Wicca
Riley Star
978-1941070130

Zombie Apocalypse
Rex Cutty
978-1941070154

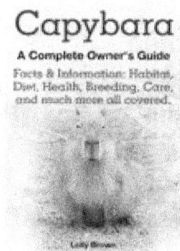

Capybara
Lolly Brown
978-1941070062

Eels As Pets
Lolly Brown
978-1941070167

Scabies and Lice Explained
Frederick Earlstein
978-1941070017

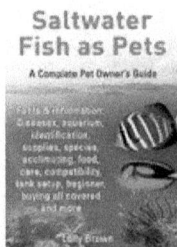

Saltwater Fish As Pets
Lolly Brown
978-0989658461

Torticollis Explained
Frederick Earlstein
978-1941070055

Kennel Cough
Lolly Brown
978-0989658409

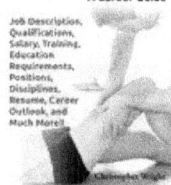

Physiotherapist, Physical
Therapist
Christopher Wright
978-0989658492

Rats, Mice, and Dormice
As Pets
Lolly Brown
978-1941070079

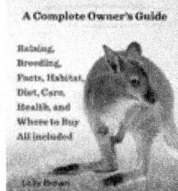

Wallaby and Wallaroo Care
Lolly Brown
978-1941070031

Bodybuilding Supplements
Explained
Jon Shelton
978-1941070239

Demonology
Riley Star
978-19401070314

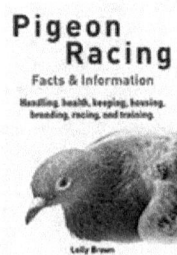

Pigeon Racing
Lolly Brown
978-1941070307

Dwarf Hamster
Lolly Brown
978-1941070390

Cryptozoology
Rex Cutty
978-1941070406

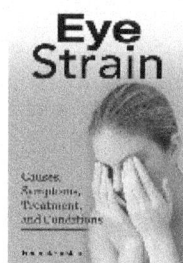

Eye Strain
Frederick Earlstein
978-1941070369

Inez The Miniature Elephant
Asher Ray
978-1941070353

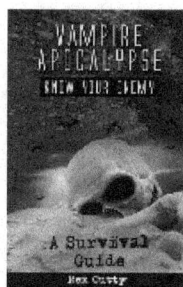

Vampire Apocalypse
Rex Cutty
978-1941070321

www.ingramcontent.com/pod-product-compliance
Lightning Source LLC
La Vergne TN
LVHW051641080426

835511LV00016B/2428